FUNDAMENTALS OF
MAINSTREAM BUDDHISM

by
ERIC CHEETHAM
BOOKLET No. 2

THE BUDDHIST SOCIETY
LONDON

MAINSTREAM SERIES

Front cover design based on Stupa found near Taxila
"A Guide to Taxila" Plate No XVII
by Sir John Marshall

Foreword

This series is intended to lead us deeper into Buddhism, and while the first booklet set the stage, so to speak, this one now acquaints us with the founder. The erstwhile Prince Gotama became the ascetic Gotama, and on awakening from the delusions that beset us human beings, was the Buddha, the Awakened One — all-wise and all-compassionate in consequence. Wherefore he spent the rest of his life teaching the way of release to like-minded others. This way is the way out of suffering, and as that is the grand theme, the grand message of Buddhism — whether played on a solitary reed-flute or fully orchestrated into great symphonies.

Westerners responding to these melodies and their message do well to acquaint themselves with the 'key' in which the music is composed. For it is other than, and foreign to, our way of thinking. The great mono-theistic religions of the West have either crumbled at the advent of science, or turn their back to time and development and retreat into fundamentalism. Being 'book'-religions, their dogmas and commandments were revealed, once and for all, by the divinity who is also the sole creator of all that is and transcends his creation absolutely. This imprint has shaped the very ways we think and perceive, and is reflected in the very structure of our languages. In Western religions, 'historicity' is an essential feature because divine revelations is to be believed to the letter! 'The book says . . .'

This is utterly foreign to Buddhism which, in common with other great Eastern religions, knows of no sole, divine, transcendent creator. In Buddhism, the sense of divinity — if so called — is seen as inherent in all that is, as the ground of all being, Buddha-Nature, Nirvana. These, and other such terms in the great orchestration stand for something that itself is beyond expression. To be re-linked with it — this again the ground-theme — leads out of suffering, out of this our world of Samsara.

The Buddha was a historical person — which is neither here nor there, for historically we know nothing about him. The manifold legends of the traditions proclaim the message against a historical setting often emphasized in detail to the extent no single historical person would encompass. Moreover, these details show a remarkable similarity to some — but by no means all — features of other great religious founders or culture-bringers.

Eric Cheetham states he is telling the story in the manner of a story-teller — and he proves himself an inspired as well as a learned one. For what the 'life' of the Buddha spells out, is not — repeat not — the authenticated biography of a historical person, but a map indispensible for the stages of the Way that is to be trodden — and has been so trodden by his followers, the greatest of whom have from their vista compassionately worked on this map and so corroborate or specify in more detail.

What Mister Cheetham presents in his booklets is main-stream Buddhism, that is to say traditional teachings basic to all schools of Buddhism, whether of the southern or northern persusasion. In these booklets he is not concerned with the local variations of one of the various schools, not held in common by all the others. Though of interest, yet again as Westerners we need to be careful with such 'individual' variations for many of them are meant to be evocative rather than factual. One such local variant for example tells of the Buddha taking leave of his distraught parents — rather than the main-stream rendering of his leaving secretly. Though the former may seem more likely to a 20th century Western mind, but in context at the time and place, even minor oriental potentates had their own ways of attaining their ends — and these did not include tearing out handfuls of their own hair! Better go secretly. Anyway, we do not know — and it does not matter. The message is clear — the inner ripening of great resolve against all odds — and the heart-searching and heart-ache that go with it.

So we have to learn to look at the traditional versions of the life of the Buddha as a 'legend' that enables us to intelligently read the map of that Way of which he had said himself that he had but re-discovered an ancient Way leading to an ancient City. It being rediscoverable — and now, thanks to the Buddha a way mapped and sign-posted — it is up to us whether we learn to read the 'legend' aright rather than getting side-tracked. 'Buddhism' is a welter of scriptures of bewildering multiplicity. Though all are orchestrations of a ground-theme (or they would not be 'Buddhist'), faced with the manifold variations we need help in finding this ground-theme against which to check not only our own favourite melody but, more important, our own steps on the Way.

So the import is whether on hearing it, one of the variations of this ground-theme touches our heart and incites us to 'follow the Way'. Hence the many variations, the many 'keys' of the Buddhist orchestration of the Way.

Myokyo-ni

FUNDAMENTALS OF MAINSTREAM BUDDHISM
Booklet No 2

Contents

Acknowledgement

*The author wishes to express his
gratitude to John Swain for the drawings
contained in these Booklets.*

INTRODUCTION

In this, the second of the Booklet series there are two principal subjects; the Life of Sakyamuni Buddha in Part I, and the first of the teaching expositions in Part II. As in the first Booklet the material is drawn from Sanskrit and Pali sources which in combination can be regarded as representing early Indian Buddhist convictions about the Biography and the Teaching which derive from the most ancient oral traditions.

Although no footnotes or other technical apparatus is provided a substantial list of additional source books is supplied. These, together with the Works of Reference in Booklet No. 1 (page 14) will give the interested reader plenty of avenues for further investigation if desired. It should be understood however that the titles listed are those actually used in the composition of the Booklets. They can by no means be regarded as a full bibliography for the subject.

There is a widespread notion among Western students and practitioners of Buddhism that the Life of the Buddha is only of passing interest compared to the need for practical application of his teachings. Whilst this is true in the narrow sense that mere curiosity about the events of long past history brings nobody any nearer to the ultimate goal of release from suffering, this view is at odds with the belief and practices of the early followers of the Dharma in India. For them it is clear from their literature and their monuments that the events of the Life were constantly remembered and contemplated. Indeed there are strong reasons for thinking that the traditional versions of the Biography formed an integral part of the Teaching and in certain respects influenced the way that Teaching was interpreted. It is only when the traditional elements of the Buddha's life story are presented as they were given that this aspect can be appraised. So it must be repeated that the selection of various oddments from the story and the discarding of what seem to us legendary intrusions deprive us of the meaning and import which only emerges from the whole. Those readers who have hitherto had the barest minimum of knowledge concerning the Buddha's life and activities may be surprised to find a wealth of instruction in the following presentation. To facilitate this perception the author has adopted the role of an ancient story teller who, without disturbing or embellishing the story itself, pauses from time to time to draw attention to relevant features.

Similar considerations apply to the fundamental teachings which begin in Part II of this Booklet. The aim is to preserve as much as possible of the original modes of expression. A fruitful re-interpretation in modern terms and for modern conditions is only likely if we know with some accuracy what was really talked about and explained by the ancient Masters. It is they, after all, who knew what was necessary to come to grips with what the Buddha taught.

Additional Works of Reference.

a) *Primary Sources.*
   i.   The Life of Buddha as Legend and History, by E.J. Thomas, London 1949.
   ii. Buddhist Scriptures, by E. Conze, (Penguin), Harmondsworth 1959.
   iii. Buddhism in Translations, by H.C. Warren, (Harvard Oriental Series) Cambridge, Mass. 1906.
   iv. Le Concile de Rajaghra, by J. Przyluski, Paris 1926.
   v.   Early Buddhist Scriptures, by E.J. Thomas, London 1935.
   vi. Buddhist Texts through the Ages, by Conze, Horner, Snellgrove and Waley, Oxford 1954.

b) *Secondary Sources.*
   i.   La Vie du Bouddha, by A. Foucher, Paris 1949.
   ii. Philosophies of India, by H. Zimmer (edited J. Campbell) London 1951.

PART ONE

THE LIFE OF SAKYAMUNI BUDDHA: THE TRADITIONAL ELEMENTS

1) *Preparations in the Past.*

From what has been set out in the first booklet of this series, on Samsara and Rebirth, it will be understood that the appearance of a Buddha in the world is an event which has occurred before and will again. Even so the vast stretches of time involved in each of the kalpas means that although one thousand successive Buddhas will appear in our present favourable kalpa there are long intervals between these Buddhas when the Teaching has died out and nothing of it remains. If we recall that one kalpa lasts for over 300 million years, even a succession of one thousand Buddhas, equally spaced, would produce intervals of 300 thousand years between each. Given that the Teaching of Sakyamuni Buddha will decline in three equal stages of 500 or 1000, perhaps even 5000 years we are still left with a minimum 'empty' period after his teaching has disappeared of 285000 years. Even if we assume that the Bhadra (favourable) kalpa refers to an 'antarakalpa' of only 16 million years (see Booklet I p. 24) one of the empty intervals between Buddhas and their Teaching is large enough to swallow all of our recorded history and Prehistory as well. This would be the minimum case of 1000 Buddhas appearing successively over 16 million years, producing equal gaps of 16000 years. The three stage decline of the Dharma after each Buddha in, say, 1000 year stages would leave us with intervals of 13000 years with no Dharma at all. It is notoriously difficult to be precise in matters of this kind and even in the two possibilities given above there are unanswered questions e.g. are we right to assume *equal* intervals between each Buddha? Whatever the right calculations may be, of one thing we can be certain, all the authorities affirm that there are enormous stretches of time during the life of a world-system when no Buddhas appear and no Dharma at all survives from the previous dispensation. In such a perspective the ancient texts do not exaggerate when they tell us that the appearance of Buddhas is a rare event, and to live in an era when their Teaching is accessible is equally rare.

There is another aspect of this rarity. The attainment of Buddhahood is not a matter of a single lifetime's effort. As we shall see, Sakyamuni attained full Enlightenment at about the age of 35, having begun his homeless life about 6 years earlier. We would be very much mistaken however, if we imagined that Enlightenment was gained by this Indian prince of rather sensitive nature but determined character, in a mere seven years of even the most arduous and dedicated striving. No real understanding of the final achievement of Enlightenment is possible unless the immense preparation over aeons of time is taken into account. The beginning of the chain of events and experience which culminated under the Bodhi tree goes back, not just beyond our present kalpa, but beyond the origin of the present world-system of 3 kalpas. The explanatory works of Indian Buddhist masters make it plain that at least three incalculable aeons are required to bring to proper maturity a being capable of full and complete Enlightenment. An incalculable aeon (asamkheya kalpa) they describe as a period required for the appearance of at least 75000 Buddhas. And it takes three of these! Sakyamuni himself emphasised this when recounting how he gained the first of the special super-knowledges of his Enlightenment. In the Pali account of the Majjhima Nikaya he says;

". . . I remembered my former existence such as one birth ((up to)) a hundred thousand births; many cycles of dissolution of the universe, many of its evolution, many of its dissolution and evolution . . ."

Armed with some idea of what is involved in these "cycles" (see Booklet No. 1) we have an appreciation of the immensity of time and of past experience intended to be conveyed. This is just one of the awesome powers of an Enlightened Buddha, and examples of his immense 'hindsight' are recorded throughout the range of the ancient texts. All of this gives us to understand that the attainment of full and perfect Enlightenment by each successive Buddha is the crowning achievement of a vast and immeasurable sequence of existences all intent upon the ultimate goal and all advancing toward it over enormous tracts of time and through unnumerable forms and stages of life. Perhaps the most striking example of one of the earliest stages of this grand march up the evolutionary scale is the occasion when Sakyamuni Buddha explained why he sometimes smiles. After observing the activity of certain insects he said;

"From generation to generation I have hitherto been a poor little insect, but little by little I accumulated good roots and I have now attained to the great wisdom and I have become a Buddha . . . All beings can also become as I am". That is why the Buddha smiled.

A whole corpus of very ancient texts called Jatakas have been put together from the scattered anecdotes of Sakyamuni's previous existences. In these Sakyamuni tells how he was once:- a lion, elephant, monkey, antelope, peacock, hare, a dog and other animals; all the time accumulating 'good roots'. These stories have sometimes been described by western writers as mere legend for the entertainment and edification of illiterate peasantry. Doubtless they were so used, but they also formed part of the well understood progress of a being who, from the most far reaching depths of time moved on, existence after existence, toward that final consummation under the Bodhi tree.

It is against such a background that the life story of Sakyamuni Buddha should be seen. Indeed it is only within such a context that all the traditional elements of that life can be understood in their true light. As we proceed to unfold the recorded sequence of those events this background should be borne in mind. In so doing many of the so-called legendary and mythical parts of the story may reveal their intended implications and as a consequence the Life will be seen to be not just history but sacred biography which is an entirely different matter.

2) *The Lineage of previous Buddhas*

We see then, that many Buddhas have appeared before Sakyamuni and many will follow him. In certain of the older texts we find 8 Buddhas mentioned by name i.e. Dipamkara, Vipasyin, Sikhin and Visvabhu of an earlier kalpa and another 4 in the present kalpa so far i.e, Krakucchanda, Kanakamuni, Kasyapa and the latest, Sakyamuni. In other texts 25 previous Buddhas are named including Pusya and an ancient Sakyamuni of a long past kalpa.

It is in the time of a previous kalpa, during the life of the Buddha Dipamkara that a crucial point was reached in the development of the being who eventually became our Buddha, Sakyamuni. The story is told in several texts but the Indian teacher Asvaghosa (c. 2nd. cent. A.D.) gives much of the detail in his work called the Buddhacarita. The outline of the incident is that a wandering scholar called Megha (sometimes Sumedha) came to the city of Dipavati. He found it in festive array and enquired what the city was celebrating. The citizens told him they were awaiting the arrival of the Buddha Dipamkara who was just then about to enter the city on a visit. Megha, who had never heard of a Buddha before was strangely moved by this news and so bought some flowers to present as an offering and joined the throng already gathered to welcome this Buddha. Soon there were welcoming cries from the onlookers and Megha then saw the Buddha Dipamkara walking slowly down the street towards where he waited. The serene majesty of that Buddha's appearance with a strange glowing light playing about his whole body impressed Megha greatly. At once Megha conceived the idea of becoming like him. Just as Dipamkara came within reach Megha and other onlookers threw their flowers in front of him intending to strew his path. But all those flowers remained hovering in the air above that Buddha's head. At the sight of this prodigy Megha pushed through the crowd and threw himself at Dipamkara's feet causing him to pause. With his long hair Megha reverently wiped the Buddha's feet and formed an ardent wish that he too would become such a Buddha. Dipamkara looked down at the prostrate form of Megha and in a moment perceived, with his Buddha powers, the whole of Megha's past lives and future births. The Buddha smiled and with Megha bowed at his feet in the dust of the road he announced to the crowd that this young student would, in aeons to come, become another Buddha with the name of Sakyamuni. Nothing more is recorded of Megha after that but this event became the archetype of the prediction of Bodhisattvas to future Buddhahood and many examples of Sakyamuni's predictions of others occur in the Mahayana sutras. According to one ancient source this city of a past aeon called Dipavati became known in Sakyamuni's time as Nagarahara sited near the modern city of Jelallabad in Afghanistan.

3) *The ripening of the Bodhisattva destined to
become the Buddha Sakyamuni.*

From the moment of his prediction by Dipamkara the student Megha was launched on a trail of exertions and trials over a whole incalculable kalpa. Thenceforward he always gained a human birth and never again fell into the lower realms of existence. Many of the human Jataka tales belong to this immense period devoted to perfecting the moral virtues. For example to perfect the quality of giving (dana) he;—

— as Prince Visvantara gave away his family and kingdom at Varsapura.

— as King Sibi gave his flesh to save a pigeon at Girarai.

— as Candrapabha gave his head at Taksasila.

— as Prince Mahasattva gave his body to the hungry tigress on the upper Indus.

Then to perfect the quality of patience (ksanti) he:-

— as Ksantivadin silently endured having all his limbs cut off by an enraged king at Mangalapura.

To fulfil the perfection of energy he visited a Buddha of the past called Pusya then residing in a mountain cave. Standing outside for seven days and nights on one leg, he praised that Buddha continuously in spontaneous verses.

Finally, under the Buddha Kasyapa of the present kalpa he lived out his penultimate existence as the ascetic Jyotipala before gaining the Tusita heaven as a fully matured Bodhisattva. There he awaited the ripening of causes and conditions on Earth before selecting the time and place for his final birth. Then he would achieve full and perfect Enlightenment and become the Buddha Sakyamuni and so fulfil Dipamkara's prediction of a previous era . . . it is only at this point that the story of our historical Buddha can rightfully commence. It is only when we are aware of the immense pre-history which brings to fruition a truly purified and vastly experienced being that the story of 'our' Buddha's life can be fully appreciated.

Before we start that story notice the succession of previous Buddhas (in section 2) all of whom are to be understood as having travelled a similar path to Sakyamuni's. Our position today within this vast framework means that many hundreds of Buddhas are yet to appear to arrive at the full quota of 1000 Buddhas for the current kalpa. That being so and given that each Buddha is preceded by infinitely long lines of development and training, then the seeds and elements of at least some of those future Buddhas are around us *now*. Certainly while Sakyamuni's Teaching dispensation lasts there is opportunity and necessity for those already existing 'lines of development' to intensify their practices and experience. The next Buddha-to-come, Maitreya, is said even now to reside in the Tusita heaven waiting, as Sakyamuni did before him, for the proper time and place for his final birth. For such a great number of forthcoming Buddhas to be sustained there must, somewhere in the world, be a being approaching the stage of Jyotipala, i.e. the human birth just before entering the Tusita where he will gain the place vacated by Maitreya when he assumes his final form. In like manner there needs to be a Megha and others suitably advanced to receive Maitreya Buddha's prediction in due time. All this flows from gaining an approximation to the original perspective of Sakyamuni Buddha's biography. So, having got such a perspective into view let us proceed with the story as provided for us by the ancient literature in both Sanskrit and Pali.

4) *The birth and youth of Sakyamuni Buddha.*

Both sets of ancient records are in close agreement on the events and manner of Sakyamuni's birth. The story begins in the Tusita heaven where the great Bodhisattva examined the world below to select the proper time and place for his final birth. He decided upon the city of Kapilavastu, capital of the Sakya clan, the site of which has been identified in North East India on the borders of Nepal. The king or chief of the Sakya clan named Suddhodana and his wife Maya were then chosen as fitting parents. Then the great Bodhisattva descended from the Tusita heaven, fully conscious and aware and entered Maya's womb. Certain accounts tell how the great Bodhisattva adopted the form of a white elephant which appeared to Queen Maya in a dream and entered her womb through her side. Her pregnancy ran the normal course except that the baby was fully equipped with all his limbs and sense organs throughout the gestation period. As the time for birth approached Queen Maya was travelling with her retinue and rested a short way from the capital in a pleasure park called Lumbini. There, standing under a tree and holding to a branch for support the birth took place. The great Bodhisattva emerged from her right side without causing his mother any pain or discomfort. As he emerged four gods from the Brahma heavens received him into a net and presented him, standing, to his mother. Two streams of water poured from the sky onto mother and child as a token of purification though neither was stained with any impurity. While the gods held a white parasol over him and carried for him other symbols of royalty, the new-born child walked seven steps toward the North and said in a loud voice that this was his last birth into the world. Modern scholars have calculated that this birth took place about the year 563 B.C. Ancient traditions from Sri Lanka (Ceylon), China and Tibet maintain variant dates, some of them considerably earlier.

Very shortly after giving birth Queen Maya died and was reborn into the Trayastrimsa heaven. Her sister Mahaprajapati took over care of the child and brought him up as her own. He was given the personal name of Siddhartha and had the family name of Gautama.

When the child was born an ascetic called Asita, dwelling in the Himalaya mountains, perceived by his supernatural powers that the gods were raising an extraordinary commotion, waving their garments and rejoicing. Seeking the cause of this celestial delight he surveyed the area with his special vision and soon perceived the shining brilliance surrounding the new-born child at

Kapilavastu. Asita decided to go and visit him. After travelling to the capital and being received with respect by the king, Asita asked to see the child who was just then asleep. As if aware of an important visitor the baby awoke and was picked up by his father to show to the visitor. With his supernatural power of vision Asita immediately saw that the child's body was endowed with the 32 special marks of a great man as well as the 80 minor marks. He therefore venerated the child by bowing and walking around him clockwise. Then he took the child in his arms and stood in silent contemplation. The king and his courtiers were then astonished and distressed to see the old ascetic begin to shed tears. At this the king became alarmed and asked the meaning of such grief. Did this portend some calamity for the boy in the future? Not at all, Asita replied. This child has only two possible destinies. If he remains a householder he will become a world emperor (Cakravartin); if he takes up the homeless life he will become a fully Enlightened Buddha who will lead countless beings to salvation. Asita himself wept because although his proficiency in the higher meditational practices assured him of rebirth in the Brahma-heavens, he would pass away before hearing and being able to follow the supreme doctrine that this new Buddha would preach. On being questioned how he was sure of the prediction Asita enumerated the 32 and the 80 special marks he could see that the child possessed and which testified to his enormous accumulation of meritorious acts in past existences. The volume and quality of the signs were such that they confirmed that the child was a special being in his last birth and with only two possible destinies. In the various texts there follow lists of these special marks which for brevity's sake are not reproduced here. A few can be given from each group and from these it will be seen that some are rather strange. Among the 32 major marks there are:-
— a protuberance on the top of the head.
— his hands hang to his knees when standing up straight
— the palms of the hands and soles of the feet are marked with wheels of 1000 spokes.
— his fingers and toes are webbed or netted.
— he has a long and very large tongue.
— there is a curled white hair between the eyebrows.
   Among the 80 minor marks are:-
— the whole body emits light.
— the eyes are large, long and the colour of a blue lotus.
— all the hairs of the head coil like a conch.
   So the king was reassured and after producing suitable gifts to Asita the ascetic departed for his hermitage in the Himalayas.
   Only two major incidents are preserved about the boyhood of Prince Siddhartha and it is uncertain in what order they occurred. Taking what is perhaps the best known first, we find the young boy in the care of his nursemaids accompanying his father to a state ritual. One source describes this

as a ceremonial ploughing of the land by the king to ensure good crops. While this is in progress the boy was placed under a shady tree and his attendants leave him alone to go and watch the spectacle. The quiet and the rare solitude are used by Siddartha to sit up straight on his cushions and observe his own breathing. Without effort or instruction he soon attained one of the meditative absorptions (dhyana) and he remained motionless and recollected throughout the whole time he was unattended. Evidently several hours elapsed because the sun moved around and the shadows cast by the surrounding trees moved accordingly. However, when his minders returned they found him still deep in meditation and protected by the shade of his tree which had not moved. All were astounded by the miraculous event and they hurried to tell the king the news. Of course the king was both pleased and disturbed because he recalled the prediction made by Asita.

The second boyhood incident is the occasion when he was taken to the local temple. This may have happened when he was quite young. In any case he could by then converse and he was taken there by his aunt and foster mother Mahaprajapati. It seems that such a presentation of young children at the temple was a custom of the time and place and may have been a form of ceremonial seeking the blessing of the gods and inviting their protection for the prince. During the preparations the boy asked his aunt where they were going. He was told he was to enter the temple and pay the customary respect and honour to the gods. To the discomfiture of his aunt the boy smiled and replied that he had already been acknowledged by the gods as their superior and entitled to their respect but that he was quite willing to go in conformity with custom. So they went but the moment Siddhartha's feet crossed the threshold of the temple all the images of the gods including Siva, Brahma and Sakra assumed bodily forms, came down from their shrines and offered praise to the boy Bodhisattva.

Before moving on to the next stage of the story it is worthwhile to pause and note certain significant features. If we are to understand from the story so far that everyone in the entourage either witnessed or knew about the unusual circumstances of the child's birth and took seriously the predictions of Asita it was surely clear from the beginning that this was a birth of great moment. His family and retainers were thus aware of the child's special status and exalted destiny. The accounts also make it clear that at this point the child Siddartha himself retained some of the characteristics of his former pursuits and was conscious of what he really was and had been. On the other hand, the special bodily marks perceived by Asita were evidently invisible to others and by their nature were not fully developed in a young child. At first then, it was common knowledge that Siddartha was far more than a son of his father and no doubt Suddhodana wanted and expected the boy's destiny to be that of a world ruling emperor.

5) *Early life of pleasure and marriage*

King Suddhodana was at pains to make sure that his son's destiny should be that of royal power and so he took care that the boy should have no wish to leave home. His father provided the youth with three separate palaces in which he spent the varying seasons of the year. His food and garments were of the very finest and even his retainers and servants were fed luxuries unheard of by the commonality. Each of the palaces was filled with precious things and he was pampered and entertained by a host of female musicians and concubines. In short, all the pleasures of the arts and the senses were at his disposal and there is nothing in the accounts to suggest that he did not drink his fill of everything provided.

Only one thing was forbidden him. He was never allowed to leave his palaces and go at will among the people and the city. Not that there was evidence of any inclination to do so. Thus for the years prior to manhood he seemed totally preoccupied with his own pleasure and the company of his personal retainers and servants. The time came when his father considered he should marry and so Suddhodana invited all the nearby princes and aristocratic families to propose their daughters for matrimonial (and of course, political) alliance. But the neighbouring peoples had a poor opinion of this prince who displayed no interest in the manly arts and who devoted his time to idle luxury and dalliance. How could one so cosseted and confined to the company of women and servants be expected to lead a kingdom and defend it from its enemies? So ran the general opinion and no ladies of rank were offered. The king was quite downcast and humiliated and asked his son whether he could demonstrate any skills in the warrior arts. To this the prince replied that he could show his ability with the great bow. When it was brought to him it was unstrung and it normally required the combined effort of several strong men to string it ready for use. With apparent ease the young prince strung the bow unaided and then struck the taut string with a stick. The resulting sound reverberated through the city and caused consternation among the populace. After this the prince accompanied his father to the practice butts and showed his prowess in shooting with the great bow so that the citizens could be assured that he was more than proficient in the arts of war. Thereafter fears for his competence were allayed and numerous ladies of rank were suggested as candidates for marriage with the prince. Of all the candidates Yasodhara was chosen and she married Siddhartha and became his chief consort. Some versions of the story name her as Gopa or Gopaka but in any case she and all the ladies of pleasure provided the prince with a life of luxurious sensual pleasure untouched by any of the cares and anxieties of the world. So passed the prince's early manhood until he was about 28 or 29. Then, as he showed no sign at all of embarking on his true destiny the gods decided to intervene.

6) *Intervention of the gods and the Great Renunciation.*

It came about that the prince began to feel restless confined to his palaces. He therefore proposed a pleasure excursion to a royal park on the outskirts of the city. The king, his father, agreed but ensured beforehand that all cripples, beggars and other afflicted persons were removed from the streets and that the route was swept clean and lined with happy people demonstrating affection for his son. Riding in the state chariot and accompanied by his charioteer, the prince emerged from his palace and rode along the streets to the delight of the populace. At this point the gods arranged for one of their number to assume the guise of an old and decrepit man. As the princely chariot progressed through the city this apparition came into full view of the prince and his charioteer. Siddhartha saw the bent and trembling figure, grey haired and hobbling along grasping a stick for support. The prince was struck with astonishment because never before had he seen anyone of advanced age and infirm with years. Turning to his charioteer he asked what sort of person this was. On being told that this was a case of age and infirmity and that it was the common lot of all, the prince was suddenly aware that old age awaited everyone. He grieved that the people should be in such festive mood despite the evidence of their ultimate fate. Deeply perturbed he abandoned his drive to the park and returned quickly to the palace. His father, surprised at the sudden return of his son enquired the reason. On learning what had happened he resolved to make redoubled effort to avoid any repetition that might turn his son's mind from the pleasures of home life.

The gods however, had taken a decisive hand in the affair and after a while they aroused in the prince's mind the desire to travel again. On two further occasions Siddhartha went out into the city with his charioteer and on each journey the gods produced an apparition that he could not avoid seeing. Once it was a sick man, unable to walk, being carried along crying in pain and anguish. After that it was a corpse, lifeless with the pallor of death, being borne along to the funeral pyre. Each time there were the same astonished shock, the questions, the sudden turning around of the chariot and flight back to the palace in alarm and agitation.

From then on he took no delight in the favors of his women attendants nor even much interest in the fact that his wife was far advanced in pregnancy. All was blighted by his sudden perception that the beauty of women and the strength of men were doomed always to the shambles of wasting age, disease and death. His thoughts began to turn toward the idea of abandoning all to search for a cure for this universal affliction. Much oppressed by these sombre reflections he decided on another chariot ride for some diversion in the open air. For the fourth time he and his charioteer ventured out into the city and this time the gods delivered the coup de grâce. They manifested a vision of a wandering mendicant who approached the chariot and on being questioned replied extolling the virtues of the homeless life, without possessions, intent only on gaining the supreme goal of final release. Once more the prince turned the chariot around but this time he had seen a practical example of an alternative life. Pondering deeply he returned to the palace and, quite exhausted, fell upon his bed and slept. When he awoke he looked around at his female attendants who, relieved for a while from the perpetual task of diverting and entertaining their lord, had fallen into a relaxed stupor. Caught off-guard the prince saw them unobserved and they presented a picture of motley disarray. All had slumped down where they were in unaffected positions of bodily exposure and in a dishevelled state. Siddartha, in an unusual mood of high sensitivity was revolted by what appeared to him as a disgusting exhibition and at that moment all desire died. As if to press home an advantage, news was just then brought to him that Yasodhara had given birth to his son. Immediately he made his resolve to abandon the home life before his new-born son added to the bonds of affection and involvement.

Calling his charioteer to saddle his horse the prince paid a last visit to his wife and son. Both were asleep so he quietly and at length gazed on them both. Then he went down to the courtyard to mount his horse and depart. The faithful charioteer insisted on going with his master and refused to be disuaded. At this point two opposing celestial powers exerted their influence simultaneously. First came Mara, the god of desire and death, who promised that within seven days the prince would become a world ruling emperor if only he stayed where he was. Briefly and impatiently the prince refused. Mara then promised he would henceforth follow him like a shadow awaiting the first moment of weakness to confound him. Other gods then put all the palace guards to sleep, muffled the horse's hooves and silently opened the palace gates letting the prince go forth in what has become known as the Great Renunciation.

Again a moment's pause is appropriate to ponder these events, for without doubt we are involved here, not only in historical events but also in religious or sacred drama. And like all sacred drama the purpose has several strands. In addition to our growing acquaintance with the story of the great Bodhisattva in his last earthly life we also see that gods of the higher realms are actively involved in that story, for and against. This is where the dramatic range is spread out to include beings of the world-system at large and so some of the elements of the Life become loaded with extra significance.

To start with, recall how the child and youth is aware of his special powers and destiny while the young man and husband seems to lose sight of it. The combined effects of his enforced isolation from the everyday world and his total immersion in sensual pleasure plus a luxurious, indolent mode of life, was only too successful. The prince in his gilded cage seems to suffer a memory blank. It were as if all his sensitivities, feelings and capacities were totally absorbed admitting no interest or concern other than his own pleasure and the continuous round of 'art'-ful engagements.

The various accounts of Asita's prediction allow the conclusion that there was enough uncertainty between the alternatives to convince the boy's father that if only the desire to leave home could be averted in his son, then the favoured destiny would ensue. The god Mara's last-minute attempt to head the prince off serves to confirm that then there really were two alternatives. If the achievement of Buddhahood had been a certainty and understood to be so by his family then the elaborate attempts to guide him away from it would have been pointless.

Then there is the intervention of the gods. As mentioned above, Suddhodana's strategy was working all too well. Note it well; even a being of such vast maturity and dedication as this great Bodhisattva seems to have been hypnotized by the concentrated dazzle of a one-sided display of Samsara's beauty and delight to the senses. We should certainly not overlook that it took four separate visions produced by the gods, each vision more powerful than its predecessor to shake the great Bodhisattva out of his stupor of contented lethargy. It is entirely proper to wonder what might have happened without such a drastic intervention by the gods. The idea serves to emphasise how necessary their intervention was.

We are thus left in no doubt as to the difficulty of turning 'against the stream' and of the immense binding power that Samsara exerts, even for beings having the skill and equipment for striving against it amassed over aeons of experience. Here it can be seen that a combination of necessary ingredients is indispensable. A perfect coincidence of causes (the Bodhisattva's innate merit and power) and of ambient conditions (the god's attentive following of events and their positive assistance) are required to bring about an end result which has been in the making for ages.

Of course there are other ways of interpreting these events. The early Mahayana view, expressed in the Suramgamasamadhi sutra has it that the great Bodhisattva at this time, i.e. before the 'shock' of the Four Signs, was already perfectly enlightened and was merely acting out an elaborate charade for the purpose of 'ripening' beings. Some of the higher gods were fully aware of this 'deception'. As they said: "the Bodisattva is not really attached to royalty and pleasure, even now he causes the Wheel of the Law to turn."

Whichever way we are inclined toward, the events are clearly meant to convey a significance beyond what is required to make the story intelligible. The opinion of the Mahayana sutra is a case in point. This is yet another reason for not tampering too drastically with the traditional elements of this biography, and for not using bits and pieces tailor-made to suit the modern view of the possible and the impossible.

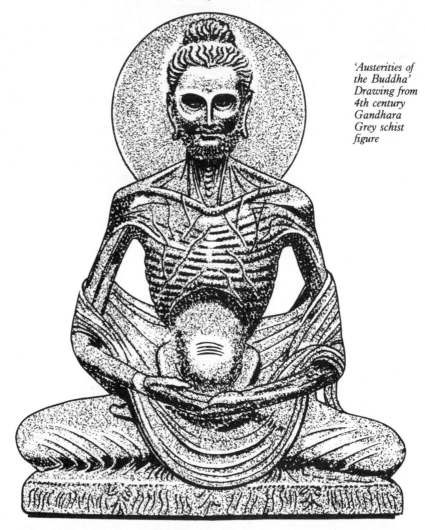

'Austerities of the Buddha' Drawing from 4th century Gandhara Grey schist figure

7) Teachers, austerities and Enlightenment.

On leaving the palace Siddhartha and his charioteer travelled south-eastwards into the night. At a distance safe from pursuit they stopped. There the prince cut off his hair, gave his fine jewels and soft clothing to the charioteer to take back, with his horse, to Kapilavastu. Several times the charioteer tried to dissuade him from leaving home and family, but was firmly rejected. When he finally took his leave Siddhartha sent a message for his father not to grieve for him as they would quickly meet again if the goal of the conquest of old-age and death could be gained. Failure in this will mean their final separation as he will never give up. The charioteer then rode back to the palace and the prince, now shaven and simply clothed, went off in search of teachers who could help him in his quest.

There seems to have been little difficulty in finding them for the great Bodhisattva (we should no longer refer to him as Siddhartha from this point onward) soon came upon a body of wandering disciples lead by their master. He is named in the Pali version as Alara Kalama. It is clear from the narrative that Alara presided over a considerable company of followers who practised a form of meditation which reached up to the highest levels of Samsara. The Bodhisattva, having approached the teacher, requested permission to join him and 'to practise the religious life' under his guidance. He was accepted and was taught Alara's system of meditation. When the Bodhisattva asked the teacher what were the limits of the meditation being taught, the answer was 'the attainment of the state of Nothingness'. Such a name is very close to that of one of the upper levels of Arupyadhatu (the Formless Realm) and is part of the topmost range of the three-tiered Indian world-system (See Booklet No. 1). However, without further ado, the Bodhisattva very soon gained both the doctrine and the practice of this meditation and was totally proficient at it. On further questioning Alara perceived that the Bodhisattva was his equal in the realisation of that doctrine and offered him the joint leadership of the company of disciples. The Bodhisattva declined. He saw that this highly refined practice had a fatal flaw. Remote from ordinary affairs it might be, peaceful it might also be, but it was still subject to unavoidable decline into decrepitude and death. So the Bodhisattva left that company and wandered on to continue his search.

Again the Bodhisattva sought out a teacher of repute. This time he attached himself to one called Uddaka Ramaputta. A similar procedure followed. First the Bodhisattva asked what the limits of the teaching and practice were. He was told it was the state of 'neither consciousness nor unconsciousness'. In fact this was one stage higher than that of his previous teacher and equivalent to the very summit of the world-system. Once again the Bodhisattva exerted his power and very soon gained the realisation of that meditation and so became the equal of his second teacher. As before, the full extent of his teacher's range was reached and still it failed to meet the ultimate criterion. A similar offer of partnership was made and declined and again the Bodhisattva abandoned the company but this time went on alone without seeking any more teachers. His wanderings led him southward into the old kingdom of Magadha and eventually to the banks of the river Nairanjana. Here he began to explore to the very limits of yoga-based experience. Here too, he was joined by five other wandering ascetics who, impressed by the strenuous nature of his efforts in yoga, stayed with him in the expectation of being the first to hear whatever revelation should eventually be revealed by this ardent practitioner.

Back in the palace at Kapilavastu, the consternation and grief can be imagined when the charioteer brought news of the prince's departure. Despite all his well intentioned efforts the king's precautions and preventive measures had failed. But the king was at least reassured that his son was well. Some of the Sanskrit sources record that he sent out messengers regularly to seek out his whereabouts and to report back with news. Later on, this thirst for tidings was to have sorry consequences, as we shall see.

Having separated himself from all teachers the Bodhisattva now embarked on the most severe practices '. . . to restrain . . . the mind . . .' He reduced his food to a single seed or grain of rice per day. He suppressed his breathing until during periods of meditation he stopped his breath completely and suffered violent pains in consequence. These extremes of self-discipline must have continued for a considerable time for he lost much of his flesh-covering and was reduced to just skin and bone. So wasted and motionless did he become that the gods, who were watching his progress intently, became alarmed at the thought that he might be dead. Other gods perceived that he was very close to death and approached him with the offer of celestial food just to keep alive. The Bodhisattva refused this because it would be a covert act and thus a falsehood. Yet the true knowledge of the deathless state eluded him. Even the very limits of yoga practice failed to produce the wisdom and insight which he sought. Then, exhausted and starved as he was, the memory came to him of the time in his early youth when he sat quietly under a tree while his father performed a state ceremonial. He recalled how, without austerities of any kind, he had attained a high degree of concentrated meditation which was devoid of all passion and distraction. It occurred to him that the better way would be in that direction. Certainly he was convinced that the most severe austerities were a dead-end and no purpose was to be served in continuing them. To do so meant certain death from debility and exhaustion, and to die meant to be reborn and so the whole sorry process would have to be repeated all over again. This new conviction decided him to take food once more to build up his strength for another approach along a different way.

It was just prior to this decision that Mara, the god of passion and death, approached him again and seeing he was close to expiry pressed him to give up the fruitless struggle and return home. With reasoning and guile Mara said that by leading a life of generosity and good deeds he could achieve both human and divine happiness. But if he persisted, Mara threatened, such an army would be raised against him that he would be utterly destroyed. The Bodhisattva knowing Mara's purpose, brushed him aside and promised Mara that soon he would conquer all of his armies and reach the supreme goal. Mara withdrew discomfited.

Then the Bodhisattva went down to the river to bathe. In his emaciated state this was a slow and painful process. Afterwards, as he made his way back up the bank to his seat he was observed by a passing peasant's daughter named either Sujata or Nandabala. Again the gods intervened and prompted her to fetch a bowl of rich milk-rice and make an offering of it to the Bodhisattva. This she did and with it he resumed taking food. His five mendicant companions on seeing this decided he had given up the struggle completely and that by taking food again after his long efforts in austerities was a signal admitting defeat. They therefore left him and continued their own wanderings. In all, this period of ascetic striving culminating in near-death and the loss of his companions lasted over six years.

After regaining his strength the Bodhisattva moved off one evening and came to the Bodhi tree where he gathered grasses and prepared his seat under its shade. On seating himself cross-legged and upright, he vowed not to arise from that seat until he had gained the supreme wisdom. Now Mara appeared to him with a whole army of terrifying monsters. Aided by his sons and daughters, all personifications of pride, lust and greed, he attempted to shake the seated Bodhisattva's resolve and then destroy him. The monsters and the rest were all launched at the Bodhisattva under the tree but none was able to reach him. Mara then challenged the great Bodhisattva to show proof of his past lineage of merit which enabled him to so disregard all the conditions and restraints of Mara's realm. The great Bodhisattva, without answering, with his right hand reached out and touched the earth on which he sat. As if in answer, the earth rumbled and roared, quaked and shook to such a degree that all of Mara's cohorts were terrified, fell to the ground and disappeared. Mara himself, repulsed and downcast, fled. But he was not yet quite done; he now resolved to distress the father of the Bodhisattva. Appearing then to Suddhodana the king, Mara offered news of his son, and then reported that the Bodhisattva had died that very day. On hearing this the king collapsed and the wives (in this version both Yasodhara and Gopaka are mentioned) sank down in tears. The king lamented that neither of Asita's predictions for the child had been fulfilled and that he had therefore lied. Once more the gods took a hand and one of them appeared to the court to announce that Asita had not lied, Mara was the liar. Indeed the king's son had just now attained to supreme and perfect Enlightenment. The king, the wives and all the inhabitants of Kapilavastu expressed great joy and the city was bedecked as if for a festival.

It was true as the gods had reported. On the dispersal of Mara and his hordes, the great Bodhisattva, as night drew on, sat undisturbed under the Bodhi tree. Deep in meditation he entered successively each of the four absorptions (dhyana). Having reached and established the fourth and highest of these meditations a series of profound insights unfolded for him. During the course of that night he at first perceived directly and clearly his own births and deaths in all his previous existences. Everything was plainly revealed in every detail from his very earliest aspirations and even his sub-human modes of life. Then, as the insight deepened, he turned his attention to the world at large. Samsara as a whole was then perceived directly with all its beings passing away here and being reborn there, according to their accumulated deeds. The entire stratified world-system from its lowest hells up to the abodes of the highest gods

*'The Buddha
as teacher'
Drawing from
4th century
Gandhara
Grey schist
figure*

appeared to him plainly "... as though reflected in a spotless mirror ..."
Finally the true nature of the world and all its beings was revealed. The causes
and hidden patterns opened out to the pure, concentrated and perfected vision
of the great Bodhisattva. These profound penetrations were later codified into
two major formulas; the Four Noble Truths and the Twelve Links of Arising
due to Conditions. The gaining of that supreme knowledge and wisdom made
the great Bodhisattva into a fully enlightened Buddha. The last stages of this
completion of an age-old path are described in some Abhidharma texts as
consisting of 34 moments of perfect vision which both stop forever the last

traces of defilement and penetrate to ultimate reality. At the same time they convey the knowledge that Buddhahood has been gained, rebirth of any kind extinguished and the Way justified.

The gods were the first to see that a new Buddha had arisen in the world and soon all the gods were rejoicing in their heavens as the Buddha Sakyamuni quietly rested under the Bodhi tree.

Ancient Buddhist commentators have long pondered, and sometimes elaborated on these momentous events. There is little doubt that the Buddha's innumerable followers down the ages are meant so to ponder them. In times past the story-tellers of Asia would have pointed out the various themes and their special significance to gatherings of illiterate but attentive listeners. Elsewhere scribes and exegetes would scratch away at their birch bark or leaves recording in erudite detail the lessons and implications of this or that part of the story. Here, all that can be done is to draw attention to some of the threads. Also, some information on the background scene of the time and place may be useful. For example the abandoning of the homelife and the search for teachers should be seen within the context of the cultural and religious ferment of the times. At this period (c. 530 B.C.) in North India, wandering mendicant teachers of religion and philosphy were commonplace. There were also several established religious sects in existence and the early Buddhist texts enumerate six different competing systems together with their leaders or principal exponents. Almost certainly there were more than this as well as innumerable individual visionaries, magicians and yoga practitioners of one sort or another. The majority were perpetual wanderers and mendicants who travelled from place to place, attracting followers here or losing them there, but all of them preached their view of the world and ultimate reality or simply entertained the locals with tricks or astounded them by their ascetic rigours. In modern times several major religio-philosophies have been identified with this milieu. Among them were the Sankhyas whose teachings derived from the already ancient Vedas and Upanishads. There were also the Jains, sometimes referred to in the Buddhist texts as the 'naked ascetics' (nirgrantha). In their case, they were a well established religious society in Sakyamuni's time with a large lay-following and their saintly leader Mahavira lived and taught at roughly the same time as the Buddha Sakyamuni.

In the northern and north-eastern areas of India, within which all these events took place, the caste system and the Brahmanical religion were not as all-pervasive as in the more westerly regions. Here, along the banks of the lower Ganges, there were a number of petty kingdoms and republics and no single religious body was predominant. Consequently, all over this vast area there were teachers of all kinds with their disciples. In general they lived an austere life of begging for subsistence or more easefully by accepting gifts from pupils or from the proceeds of public preaching or debate with opponents. The fact that the great Bodhisattva fled from home in a south-easterly direction would bring him into the heart of this domain of conflicting enquiry in more senses than one. Thus the great Bodhisattva was repeating a mode of life which he had adopted many times in his past existences e.g. as Megha at the time of Dipamkara and as Jyotipala in the life prior to his residence in the Tusita. Bearing this in mind it is not so surprising that he should very quickly master the techniques and the teachings of his two preceptors. What we seem to have here is rather in the nature of a revision or a refurbishing of skills and capacities already latent but dulled by his princely life of luxurious idleness.

With regard to the early teachers themselves, from the descriptions of their meditational practices it is likely that they were followers of the Jaina system. Both practices seem to have a remarkable similarity to the very highest levels of the commonly held world-system. And it was just this 'top of the world' which Jaina saints aimed ultimately to achieve. Not only was it to be reached in meditation but a 'pure' death was sought which would result in the saint's "life monad" rising to that summit of the world, there to remain in blissful peace for ever. In this context the great Bodhisattva is shown as gaining and discarding the most sublime achievements of his most spiritually advanced contemporaries. Some texts of the Abhidharma when explaining these matters at a later date, warn that these highest levels of Samsara attained by the practice of 'absence of perception' (asamjnisamapatti) were a dead end and a wrong path misleading even the most skilled and advanced ascetic into quiescent states which they imagined to be the final release of Nirvana which they are not.

Another feature of this sacred drama which needs to be underlined is the several interventions of the gods in this, the final stage of the Bodhisattva's career. After their crucial and decisive assistance in bringing about the Great Renunciation, in the final assault on 'the gates of the immortal', the gods are at first absent from the stage. It is as if they watched with bated breath as the great Bodhisattva approached ever nearer his goal. As impotent observers and occasional helpers they demonstrate their inferior status to the great Bodhisattva, whatever their rank in the celestial hierarchy. Once enlightened the Buddha was emphatic that he was 'the teacher of gods and men' and that he was the 'conqueror' (Jina) of birth and death and thus the whole range of Samsara. All of the gods, without exception, despite their long lives extending in some cases over millennia, yet had an end to their exalted existence when death finally over took them and they made way for another incumbent. Even so, at times their assistance was critical, though as the great Bodhisattva moved beyond their reach, towards the final achievement, it was of a more humble nature. Such were their offerings of food to alleviate the ravages of fierce self-discipline and the prompting of the girl Sujata to prepare and bring food when most needed and acceptable. Again they took care that the great Bodhisattva's family were not left in utter distress at Mara's deceitful news.

The case of Mara is quite otherwise. While the great Bodhisattva's progress took him out of reach of the gods it also brought him into progressively severe confrontation with the great god of passion and death. From efforts at subtle temptation Mara was forced into attempts to destroy the great Bodhisattva under the Bodhi tree. This increasing hostility and opposition by Mara shouldn't really surprise us. From the moment of his Great Renunciation the Bodhisattva saw clearly that it was the interminable round of death and rebirth which had to be overcome. Any other achievement, even the highest states of meditation, was still a form of bondage. Thus it is entirely fitting that the last great confrontation and trial of strength should be against Mara just prior to the attainment of Enlightenment (Bodhi). And such is the nature of Mara and what he represents that even the great Bodhisattva had to call upon all the concentrated power amassed by his innumerable past lives of effort and development and for it to manifest and subdue Mara and his minions with a literally earth-shaking surge of fully ripened and purified energy. So the last enemy having been overcome, the gates of the immortal swung open once more and the great Bodhisattva passed through to the deathless and became the new Buddha of this age.

Significantly no human eye witnessed this great event. Only the gods among all living beings knew and perceived what had taken place, and they all rejoiced. Significantly too, Mara having failed to prevent it, continued his nefarious works by attacking the only traces of the new Buddha remaining to him, the anxious, waiting family.

We can now return to the new Buddha sitting quiet but resplendent under the Bodhi tree. He still had to fulfil his promise to bring relief to the world once he had found the Way. The various traditions tell us that it was to this that the newly enlightened mind was turned during the several weeks that elapsed before the Buddha left the shade of the tree of Enlightenment.

8) *The decision on how to re-establish the 'ancient Path' in the world.*
The ancient texts provide us with slightly varying accounts of what happened next. In outline they all agree however, that there was a pause of from one to seven weeks after the attainment of Enlightenment. During that period the matter of teaching to others what was revealed by full and perfect Enlightenment was resolved. First, the new Buddha remained seated under the tree plunged into deep meditation on the true nature of things and in particular he is said to have reviewed the chain of causation or 'arising due to conditions' (pratityasamutpada) forward and backward absorbing its full import and application to all beings and circumstances. It was clear to him that his new-won true knowledge was profound, subtle, transcendent and hard to obtain. His direct perception of the capacities of ordinary people and even the extra-ordinary people showed that they were enmeshed in so many attachments,

ideas and convictions that it would be difficult for them to gain access to the real and the ultimate state. This involved the deep penetration to underlying causes and conditions and the cessation of all passions. Both of these were beyond the reach of all but the most spiritually advanced of mankind. If the Buddha himself had only gained this full Enlightenment after aeons of continuous striving and effort, how could men of the world lacking his enormous endowment of merit and wisdom be expected to understand, or even accept, a teaching of such profundity which went 'against the stream' of all worldly convictions and affairs. Thus emerged a dilemma of far-reaching importance. The tradition in the Pali texts tells us that the Buddha hesitated over whether to teach his great wisdom at all and his first reaction was to remain silent because of the 'weariness and vexation' of the inevitable misunderstandings. Other traditional versions from the Sanskrit confirm that the dilemma was there but that the great compassion for the world inherent in the Enlightenment experience itself overruled any hestitation. On surveying the world with his clear supernatural vision the Buddha could see that there were some who were less immersed in the passions than others. His supernatural vision also allowed him to see and to know that all the Buddhas of the past and those yet to come had taught and would teach the profound wisdom, and thus the decision was made.

While these deliberations were going on the gods were watching the quietly meditating figure and they wondered whether or not he would decide to teach. As time went by they became anxious and then alarmed that perhaps after all this effort and their careful ministrations the great Teacher whom they had confidently expected and identified would, in the event, turn away from the task of making known to all men that the 'ancient Path' had at last been re-discovered. Toward the end of the post-Enlightenment pause Brahma, king of the higher gods (in some accounts Indra/Sakra too) descended from his heaven realms and taking suitable form, stood before the Buddha under the Bodhi tree. With reverence and joined hands Brahma addressed the Buddha with the request that he have pity on the world and teach his new-won doctrine. Echoing some of the profound thoughts which had already occurred to the Buddha, Brahma said that there were beings of little impurity in the world who would relapse into the lower states if they did not hear and receive the Dharma now in the Buddha's power to dispense. In the Pali version it was just this request at the critical moment by the chief of the gods that overcame the Buddha's hesitation. In other versions, like that in the Buddhacarita from mainland India, Brahma's request merely set the seal on the decision already made and gave the opportunity for the Buddha to avow his intention to teach. Whichever way it was there followed the fervent utterance to Brahma that the gates of the immortal were now open and those who could hear and understand should attend to the Dharma about to be revealed. Some of the Pali accounts record that during the gestation period immediately after the Enlightenment the Buddha had devised the whole of the Abhidharma which implies that the mode and method of teaching were prepared.

Before any teaching took place however, there now appeared two travelling merchants who, together with their caravans, happened to be passing. This incident is mentioned in both sets of documents and in the Pali version they are named as Tapussa and Bhallika. The gods once more resumed their participation and prompted these merchants to approach the still seated Buddha with offerings of food. After their proffered food was accepted both merchants bowed and as if moved by the splendour and assurance of that great presence said to the Buddha that they took refuge in him and in his teachings, but omitted the third part of the Refuge formula as there was as yet no Samgha. In fact these first 'converts' received no teaching at all but were sent on their way with assurances of good fortune to come.

Now the Buddha turned his mind toward the practical problems of who could be the first to receive his teaching. Recalling first his two teachers, Alara Kalama and Uddaka Ramaputta the Buddha soon perceived that they had died. His thoughts next turned to his erstwhile followers who had abandoned him when he resumed taking food. Perceiving that they were now staying in the deer park of Isipatana at Benares he resolved that they would be his first disciples. Accordingly he then rose and left the seat of Enlightment under the Bodhi tree and made his way along the road to Benares.

The interval between the attaining of full Englightenment and the departure from the Bodhi tree perhaps contains some of the most profound implications of all the incidents in this traditional biography. In the first place it marks a boundary between the consummation of aeons of struggle and the start of what that consummation could do for the world at large. From being focused on a single exalted being moving steadily and steadfastly toward an as yet unrealized goal, the story now begins to spread out to relate how that tremendous achievement was managed and released for others capable of responding to the direct testimony of one who had 'gained the other shore'. And here indeed, at the very threshold of the Buddha's first recorded teaching, the dilemma is intense.

What is involved in the great and unsurpassed wisdom of a Buddha's full Enlightenment was clearly beyond the grasp of even the most spiritually advanced of Sayamuni Buddha's contemporaries. Had he not gained and abandoned the best that was available long before and was that not followed by six years of intensive search which took even one as greatly endowed as a Bodhisattva in last birth to the very limits of endurance? Evidently no other living being of the time could duplicate this singular attainment; an attainment, be it noted, which changed the whole being of the subject from a greatly endowed Bodhisattva Prince into a Buddha/Tathagata, knower of all the worlds throughout time, god of all gods and supreme teacher of men. It is clear from the deep considerations which took place after the Enlightenment that the awesome depth and range of the Buddha knowledge is just not transferable simply for the asking, nor can it be delivered as one might demonstrate a theorem. The situation is succinctly described in the early pages of the Lotus sutra where Sakyamuni unequivocally states that only another Buddha can fully understand a Buddha. And yet to keep his own promise and to fulfil the task of every Buddha he *had* somehow to teach and bring his rediscovery within reach of ordinary beings. No wonder the gods looked on in anxious concern while the dilemma was resolved.

So the choice of the first recipients and the substance of that first teaching are worthy of special note. As we shall see (in Part II) the content of that exposition was embedded firmly in the world as it is, as normally experienced by everyone and particularly those who already search for the real. Its general characteristic is of a mass of sustained suffering and turbulence. Nothing was said about the very essence of Enlightenment, the subtle chain of causal conditions which governs everything. Yet such was the skill of the Master that even that first teaching, addressed to the selected five, brought about their preliminary release and insight.

9) *The first turning of the Wheel of the Doctrine at Benares.*
Walking along the road to Benares the Buddha, now in his middle thirties, was seen and approached by another ascetic. He is said to have been impressed by the serene appearance of the Buddha and according to the custom and etiquette of the time the ascetic greeted him and asked what doctrine he followed and who was his teacher. At this, the Buddha, whose worldly appearance was that of a young man in the prime of life, must have astonished the enquirer who probably expected an enthusiastic account of some local teacher to whom he could go and put questions. Instead the Buddha pronounced himself beholden to no teacher but the Victor and Conqueror of all the world, superior to gods and men alike, an All-Enlightened One endowed with omniscience. This must have startled and disconcerted the ascetic for there is no hint that he could see anything of the Buddha's true nature from his appearance. He muttered something like, "if only it were true", and took himself off rather sharply, leaving the Buddha to continue his journey.

According to some of the sources this journey on foot from Bodh Gaya to Benares took eight days following the post-Enlightenment pause. Eventually the Deer Park was reached and there the five past followers sat together under the shade of the trees. In one text they are named as: Kaundinya, Mahanaman, Vaspa, Asvajit and Bhadrajit. They saw Sakyamuni coming toward them from a distance and conferred together as to how they should receive him. At this stage all five mendicants were completely unaware of the profound change which had taken place in the person they remembered. They still recalled him as the ascetic who had given up. When they saw him approach they therefore decided that he was not worthy of their respect though the courtesies of the time required that he should be conversed with if he so wished. As Sakyamuni came nearer to them they found themselves unable to maintain such a condescending attitude. Some of them prepared a seat, some placed water for his feet and others took from him his bowl and outer robe. While doing these things they addressed him by his family name of Gautama or as 'friend' and this drew a prompt rebuke. The Buddha told them it was not proper to address him by his family name, even less by the basic form of 'friend'. He said, "I am a fully enlightened Buddha, a Tathagata, and I now teach". Despite their reluctant respect the five mendicants still were unable to accept this and they reminded the Buddha that he had given up striving so how could he be believed when he now claimed to have achieved his goal. The Buddha persisted and after three such exchanges the five were convinced that here indeed was a teacher worthy of attention and reverence. Thereupon Sakyamuni Buddha made the first exposition of the new Teaching/Doctrine (Dharma) now known to us as the first turning of the Wheel of the Law. The five mendicants listened intently while the doctrine of the Middle Way was pronounced i.e. avoiding the two extremes of unrestrained passion and worldly indulgence, and of the self-torture of severe austerities. This was followed by the formula of the Four Noble Truths i.e. the universality of suffering; its cause; its termination; and the eight parts of the Way to achieve the termination of suffering. At the end of this exposition one of the five, Kaundinya, gained a pure insight into the veracity of the teaching and was praised for it by the Buddha who confirmed the attainment with the words, "Kaundinya has attained the knowledge . . ." It is not said specifically that he then attained Arhatship. Indeed the Sanskrit version maintains that Kaundinya gained what was later to become known as, 'the pure eye of the Dharma'. Certainly a period of intense instruction followed for all five because we are told that three of them went begging for food while the remaining two received instruction. All six of them shared the food received. Then the three were instructed while the two others went begging. In this way they fed themselves and received instruction until all five gained the fruit of Arhatship. All five were the first to be received into the Buddha's Order of monks; Kaundinya first, followed by Vaspa and Bhadrajit and finally Mahanaman and Asvajit. The gods, continuing to observe closely the progress of events, rejoiced and declared that the Wheel of the Dharma had indeed been set in motion once again.

The small group of disciples stayed with the Buddha at Benares for a while and soon the next recruit was gained. There lived in the city a son of a wealthy merchant called Yasa and he, out walking at night in a disturbed state of mind, came upon the Buddha in the Deer Park. This young man listened to the same recital of the Four Noble Truths by the Buddha and very soon after attained

Arhatship. Later, Sakyamuni accepted a meal at the family home of Yasa's mother and former wife and they then became lay-followers. Yasa's many friends and acquaintances, curious at the sudden conversions, came to see the Buddha and of them and their associates over 50 entered the Order and soon after instruction became Arhats. It was then, before leaving Benares, that Sakyamuni sent out 60 of the first Arhats in all directions to preach the Doctrine which they had heard and realized for themselves. This mass dispersal must have stripped the Buddha of almost his entire following of fulfilled disciples. Only Asvajit and Mahanaman and a few others seemed to have remained with him when he left Benares and turned his steps in the direction of Rajagrha, capital of Magadha.

Here we have seen a newly attained Buddha reaching out to find people suitably endowed to receive the news that the 'gates of the immortal' were open. It was a commonplace of the time that disciples sought their own masters. Sakyamuni did just that when he first left home. Now however, a unique being, a fully enlightened Buddha does not wait for people to come to him, he seeks out his first disciples. This is partly the result of the dilemma previously discussed. People would certainly come to him, they already had. The two merchants were willing supporters but they received no teaching. At this crucial beginning it seems to have been vital to select those who were capable of some understanding, willing or no.

At first we see the five 'deserters' as unwilling even to receive the new Buddha advancing toward them. It is obvious that they could not see the majestic, golden haloed figure that many would see later on. but they evidently saw a different figure from the half starved ascetic they had left in disgust. Some emanation reached them from the advancing figure which induced their deference, polite at first, compulsive soon after. And then there is the incident of the wandering ascetic who also perceived something remarkable about this young man striding out toward Benares. Again, the 'glorious body' was not in evidence, but something was and the ascetic must have been taken aback to be told by such a young man that he was above all the gods. Notice too that no teaching was given here either. The first recipients had been singled out and that was that. Even with them there was to be no nonsense about calling a Buddha by the slightly condescending title of 'friend'. That response had called forth a stern rebuff. His titles were Buddha or Tathagata and he was so addressed thereafter, otherwise as 'Lord' (Bhagavan). A proper attitude toward himself was clearly of some importance before his teaching could be dispensed. Hence the intense persuasion of the five before the Buddha taught.

As for the teaching itself, the first section of it consisted of the Middle Way between the two extremes. However we may interpret this teaching nowadays it was certainly aimed then directly and specifically at those five who held the view that the practice of self mortification was correct in its own right (they represented a large body of contemporary opinion) and to abandon it spelled defeat and consequent failure to achieve the goal of insight. One of the incidental discoveries along the great Bodhisattva's way to supreme Enlightenment was that body and mind had to be fit and healthy to sustain and support the enormous effort for Enlightenment. So here at the outset wrong attitudes had first to be corrected and direct contact with where *they* stood was necessary. It also illustrates what was to be the hallmark of all Sakyamuni's teaching technique; that the expostion had to be fitted to the listener's capacity. This too flowed from those weeks of meditation under the Bodhi tree when the dilemma of a message from beyond the world as generally known had to be conveyed intelligibly to those still in it.

Well might the gods rejoice and raise a commotion as the Wheel of the Doctrine started to turn again. And when the deceptively simple statement of the Four Noble Truths followed that of the Middle Way they knew that the Dharma was well and truly launched. Especially so when, one after the other, the five disciples gained preliminary insight and release from the bonds. These five, and soon after them numerous others gained the fruit of Arhatship and one wonders at the relative speed of such attainments. In a way, these quick successes serve as a contrast to the immeasurably higher status of the Buddha himself as compared with his Arhats. And this has always been acknowledged; that while the release and higher knowledge of Arhatship is the same for the Buddha and his disciples, even so the Buddha stands out above them all in full and supreme Enlightenment.

10) *Growth of the early Samgha and conversion of Sakyamuni's family*

The journeying on foot from place to place over long distances was typical of the Buddha's habit throughout his long life. Now, on leaving Benares for Rajagrha he would proceed by stages, stopping here and there so that the route was not always direct. As the crow flies the distance from Benares to Rajagrha is little short of 200 miles and with diversions rather longer. On just such a lengthy journey, walking the dusty track in the cool of the day, a brahmin called Dona fell in with the Buddha's travelling party. It happened that Dona found himself walking directly behind the Buddha and to his astonishment each of Sakyamuni's footprints left the clearly discernible mark of a wheel with 1000 spokes. Under normal circumstances these special bodily marks, seen for the first time by the sage Asita on the child Siddhartha's body, are largely invisible to the human eye. The strong inference is that Sakyamuni wanted them to be seen by this man. Later, when the party was resting and Sakyamuni was seated under a tree Dona approached him and asked if he were a god or a spirit. "Neither" was the reply. "Then are you a human being" asked Dona. "Indeed not" Sakyamuni replied. "Just as a lotus is born and grows in the water and mud but is unsoiled by it, just so is a Buddha."

On the journey from Benares, along the banks of a river there were several communities of religious ascetics led by the three Kasyapa brothers. Certain of the texts describe them as fire-worshippers with matted hair. In order to convert these men to the Dharma, Sakyamuni had recourse to a great array of supernatural powers. In particular he is said to have subdued local naga spirits who belched out smoke and flame at him. None of this stirred the elder Kasyapa from his beliefs. He merely acknowledged that Sayamuni was a great master of magic. However when Saymuni denied that Kasyapa's path of practice led to full attainment he began to have doubts and asked to join the Buddha's entourage. Eventually all three brothers and their combined following of 1000 entered the Order as disciples and the Buddha preached to all of them the now famous Fire Sermon. This was to the effect that all the senses and their objects are on fire with the passions of greed, hatred and delusion. Once this is known and understood aversion and disengagement arise and with that release follows. On hearing this sermon many became Arhats.

On arrival at Rajagrha, Sakyamuni and his now substantial following were met by the king, Bimbisara, and a host of citizenry. At first the populace were not sure who was the leader of the monks because of the presence of the well known Kasyapa brothers. To clarify the position the elder Kasyapa acknowledged the Buddha as Lord and teacher and then Sakyamuni preached to all including the king. Bimbisara was converted and gave to the Order the nearby Bamboo Grove.

It was near here too, at Rajagrha, that the Buddha gained his two foremost disciples, Sariputra and Maudgalyayana (Moggallana in Pali). Both were wandering mendicants searching for 'the immortal' and just then were followers of a local ascetic teacher. Each of them had assured the other that he would be the first to be told should one of them find what they looked for. While the Buddha and the Order stayed at Rajagrha, the Arhat Asvajit went out on his begging round. This was the same Asvajit who heard the first preaching at Benares. Sariputra saw Asvajit begging and was impressed by his demeanor. At a convenient pause Sariputra approached him and after the usual formal compliments asked who his teacher was and what was the teaching he followed. Asvajit replied that he followed the Lord Buddha then staying in Rajagrha, that he himself was not a skilled teacher and could only give him the essence of the doctrine in brief. He then pronounced to Sariputra a four line verse which became famous in later times. In translation it says:

"Dharmas which are born from a cause
the Tathagata has proclaimed
the cause as well as their stopping.
Thus teaches the great ascetic".

Just as in the case of Kaundinya, on hearing this a sudden insight arose in

Sariputra and he understood the universal application of arising and passing away. Another case of inducement of 'the spotless eye of the Doctrine'. After expressing his thanks and taking his leave of Asvajit, Sariputra hurried off to tell his companion that their search was ended. Both now prepared to leave their teacher and go to the Buddha. Many of their companions who heard the news decided to go with them. Sakyamuni, who saw them coming from a distance remarked to those nearby that the two who now approached would be his chief disciples.

Now the Buddha decided to return to Kapilavastu and visit his family. Journeying as usual on foot by gradual stages, he and his whole company of monks which now numbered many hundreds, left Rajagrha and headed north west across the Ganges toward the Himalaya range. On arrival the whole party was lodged at a local park but no-one offered the Buddha any particular respect. As in the case of the first five disciples, the Buddha's status seemed to need acknowledgement before fruitful teaching could take place. Here, among the Sakya clan, a people notorious in their time for pride of race and of family, something more than persuasive explanation was required. So, there and then, in front of his father and all the nobles and retainers of his home town, Sakyamuni suddenly rose into the air and performed what became known as the miracle of the pairs or of fire and water. Suspended high in the air above the astonished crowd the Buddha caused fire to burst out from the upper part of his body while sheets of water cascaded down from the lower part. Then the fire appeared from his right side and water from the left. This was repeated in a number of variations followed by the creation of a promenade of jewels in the sky along which he walked or appeared in various stances. On completing this spectacular display he descended to earth and his father and the assembled nobles bowed to him in awed respect. But no-one invited him to a meal. The next day therefore, Sakyamuni with his monks went begging for food in the city,as was normal. Everyone came out to watch the king's son, dressed in plain robes, beg from house to house like any other common mendicant. When they heard about this the king and the family, as members of the warrior caste, were scandalized and distressed. Suddhodana left the palace and sought out Sakyamuni on his round. With great respect but with firm disapproval Sakyamuni's father asked him why he was disgracing his family thus in public. Surely no-one of their royal lineage had ever begged in the streets before. At this reproof Sakyamuni replied that he was not now of that royal line. His lineage was that of the Buddha Dipamkara and others down to the Buddha Kasyapa, the last of the line before Sakyamuni. All these illustrious predecessors had begged for their sustenance and so Sakyamuni rightly conformed to the practice. At this the king was finally convinced and he became a lay-follower of his erstwhile son's Dharma. Suddhodana soon became more familiar with the members of the Order and conceived the idea that a motley crowd of errant monks of uncertain origin was no fit entourage for his son, Buddha or not. He

*'The Pillar of Fire' Detail drawing from a
3rd century Amaravati stone relief*

therefore decreed that a son from each of the noble Sakya families should join
the Order to ensure that Sakyamuni should have 'suitable' companions. In this
way an element now entered the Order, not by desire and conviction, but by
decree. Among these was Devadatta whose later activities were to cause such
dissension. Other 'entrants by order' were a number of well known relations
and kinsmen including Ananda, Nanda, Aniruddha and the barber Upali.

A special mention has to be made of his wife Yasodhara and his young son
Rahula. All the palace ladies including Mahaprajapati, Sakyamuni's foster
mother, came to see the Buddha and offer respect, except Yasodhara. She

waited for Sakyamuni to go to see her, which he soon did and in the presence of Suddhodana she paid him homage by touching his feet with her head. The king related how she had followed Sakyamuni's progress up to Enlightenment from the news brought by the messengers. Yasodhara had in fact copied Sakyamuni's mode of life to some extent by wearing yellow robes, taking only one meal a day and abandoning perfumes and adornments. Sakyamuni responded by telling of Yasodhara's devotion in previous lives as was the case for Suddhodana also. Yasodhara however, had not entirely given up the idea that this was still her husband and that he might return to her. Some of the sources tell us that she prepared a love potion in a bowl of delicious food and sent her seven year old son Rahula to the Buddha with it for him to eat. Sakyamuni, knowing this, created 500 look-alike Arhats and sat among them when the boy came. Rahula, despite this, came straight to the real Buddha without hesitation and offered him the bowl. Although the doctored food was not accepted there was no doubt that here was a son who recognised his father. On another occasion Yasodhara sent the boy to follow him to the park of residence where Saributra was told to admit Rahula as a novice to the Order. When news of this reached Suddhodana he made complaint to Sakyamuni that it was painful for parents to lose their only sons to the Order and it was especially so to him for he had now lost both son and grandson. He asked that in future no-one would be admitted to the Order without parental permission and this was agreed and remains so.

According to one reconstructed chronology several years of further wanderings were to elapse until in the sixth year after the Enlightenment the next major incident took place at Sravasti. During this interval King Suddhodhana died and Mahaprajapati, his principal widow, sought entry into the Order along with other Sakya women. The Buddha refused Ananda's pleading on their behalf until at the third request he granted it provided the ladies accepted extra strict rules which had the effect of giving them lower status than the monks. These being accepted the Order of Nuns came into being but Sakyamuni told Ananda that the result would be a shortening of the life of the Dharma in the world.

Whilst in Sravasti the Buddha stayed at the Jetavana Park recently donated to the Order by the great benefactor Anathapindika. Here, the miracle of the pairs was performed for the second time. On this occasion the whole Samgha was challenged by rival religious groups to a public display of magical prowess. Sakyamuni forbade any of his monks to so perform for this purpose but he evidently regarded the issue as sufficiently important for him to do so. Once again he entirely over-awed the crowd and his antagonists with the display of fire and water and promenading in the sky. No-one could improve on that.

It was also from Sravasti that Sakyamuni disappeared altogether from India for three months while he visited his mother in the Heaven of the Thirty-Three (Trayastrimsa). Maya had been reborn there after her early death and

*'Descent from Trayatrimsa'
Detail drawing from a 4th century Gandhara stone relief*

Sakyamuni was aware that all the previous Buddhas had been at pains to convert their parents to the Dharma. The textual sources are agreed that the Buddha spent his time in the Trayastrimsa teaching his mother the Abhidharma. Although particular teachings are not specified there is a certain significance in the fact that Abhidharma is mentioned at all at this juncture. After converting his mother, Sakyamuni performed another of those spectacular demonstrations long remembered by generations of commentators and carefully carved in stone for the edification of countless pilgrims. Instead of returning to earth at Sravasti he descended from the mountain top heaven to

Sāmkāśya, on the upper reaches of the Ganges, 200 miles to the west. And contrary to his simple ascension to the heavens, his descent was full of splendour and grand display. On the night of the full moon in October the startled people of Samkasya would have seen a triple stairway slowly descending from the cloudy heights to touch earth firmly just outside their town. Soon, to the sounds of heavenly music, the Lord Buddha could be seen descending the grand stairway made of precious metals and jewels and accompanied by crowds of the gods. On his right the Buddha was escorted by Brahma, king of the gods, and on his left was Indra/Sakra, ruler of the Trayastrimsa and the lower heavens. By the time the Buddha had stepped off the stairway to earth many of the leading Arhats in the Samgha, Sariputra at their head, had hastened there to greet and receive this royal cavalcade. According to one group of texts however, one of the principal Arhats absented himself from this celestial levée, he was Subhuti. He remained in his cave retreat near Rajagrha, absorbed in meditation on sunyata (emptiness) which he considered was the only true homage to the Tathagata. Far away at Samkasya, when Sariputra greeted the just descended Buddha in the name of the Samgha, the Buddha said that Sariputra was not really the first to receive him. It was Subhuti who performed the true homage, not those who just saluted his perceived body. Much was made of this from the earliest times when there was long pondering and discussion on the so-called Dharma-body. Such was the reverence with which this event was held that the site at Samkasya was marked with shrines and it remained one of the cardinal sites on the pilgrim's circuit of the holy places in Indian until Hsuan-tsang's time and beyond.

If we had any doubt about the unique nature of Sakyamuni before his Enlightenment, we should have none afterward. On the occasions of contact with his early followers and with casual meetings there was something mysterious about his effect on people and in his pronouncements on being superior to the gods. There was also the sensitivity about being addressed with too much familiarity. But here in the exchange with Dona when the imprint of the 1000 spoked wheel was seen on his footprints, we have an unequivocal reply to a straight question; 'Are you a human being?' Dona asked. 'No', was the reply. Neither was he a god nor any other category of being in Samsara What then was (is) the Buddha? That is a prime question with emerges from the traditional biography and it is one which exercised the minds and meditations of whole generations of Indian Buddhist masters. The answer to that question was a matter which divided whole sections of the early Samgha: the question nagged from the very beginning and one of the sets of answers helped to lay the foundations for what we now know as the Mahayana. For us now, it is enough to perceive the question itself. Any answers we arrive at will to a large degree be determined by our individual tendencies and the extent of our understanding. At least we know what he was not. The ancient texts leave little doubt as to that.

'Bodhi tree throne' Detail drawing from 1st century Sanchi stone relief

The early sculptors of India who decorated the stupas of highest antiquity such as at Sanchi and Amaravati portrayed this mysterious being with great subtlety and with striking originality. Where the Buddha was supposed to be present they indicated his presence by an empty throne, or a Bodhi tree with a seat at its foot but no seated figure, or even large footprints impressed with 1000 spoked wheels. But never with a physical form. The first images of the Buddha in India were carved centuries after the establishment of the major divisions in the Samgha.

In the same category are several other incidents in this section. The distress and perplexity of Suddhodana on seeing his son begging in the streets and Sakyamuni's categorical rejection of the ties of worldly family. His lineage is that of the previous Buddhas, none other. Similarly, his accounting for the present circumstances of Yasodhara and his father by the events of their past lives. This practice of explaining present situations by activities in the past was often resorted to for Sariputra and others and later in this biography we shall see it again on a much larger scale. In the vast over-view of the past aeons of Samsara we seem to have a situation where certain 'streams of development' ran parallel to each other for ages. So much so that the final ripening of certain actions in the past brought these parallel streams to a contemporaneous birth as the different characters of a dramatic climax — all the major characters being drawn around the central figure and all, in some way or another, dependent on him.

The descent to earth from the visit to Maya, on a jewelled stairway in majestic array attended by the gods Brahma and Sakra tells us in unmistakable terms that here is a being without equal in the entire world-system. Here at least is a positive ancient representation which should convey, by its royal trappings and its bringing together of the heavens and earth, some indication of how the Buddha and his ministry were perceived by the ancients.

11) *A long life of wandering and teaching*

Assuming what is now widely accepted as the Enlightenment taking place at the age of about 35 and death at about 80 years of age, the Buddha spent 45 years trudging the pathways and tracks of north and east India. There is plenty of recorded detail about the first years of his ministry and about the last year or so before his death, but little chronological narrative of the 35 years or so in between. Of course, all the scriptural texts give us quantities of anecdote and a mass of teaching topics which must have taken place during this long middle period. But the thread of the narrative seems to have been lost or perhaps dropped in favour of a great collection of unrelated stories and detailed expositions of doctrine and practice. This is not the place to recount all these incidents, nor is it possible without reproducing most of the canonical material. Instead, it should be understood that Sakyamuni continued his wandering, his preaching, his conversions and his instructions to the rapidly growing Order of monks and nuns.

When we stop to consider what is known of Sakyamuni's daily routine, of the extent of his travels to spread the Teaching, it should be realized that hardly a day went by during his long life span when some instruction, exposition or general preaching did not occur. Consider first the area he travelled. All the towns and villages along the middle and lower Ganges basin saw him time and again. On the left bank, the northern boundary extended from Sravasti to Samkasya, about 500 kms. On the right bank, the southern boundary went from Rajagrha and further east, to the western limit of Kausambi approx. 450 kms. The north/south axis of the territory was at least 400 kms. wide. This enormous area was traversed many times in the course of decades of peregrinations. It is recorded that, apart from the months of the rainy season when the whole Order stayed put wherever they happened to be, the rest of the year was spent visiting one place after another, mostly on foot, but sometimes on the river. This perpetual movement during the larger part of every year must have taken up a substantial part of many a day's routine. It is clear though, that stops were made of varying length at places of particular importance like the Kosalan capital at Sravasti, the Maghadan capital at Rajagrha and the capital of the Vrjjian republic at Vaisali.

The regular features of the daily routine other than travel were; the begging round, bathing and meals, the twice daily 'survey of the world' with his supernatural vision, preaching as thanks after an invited meal, instructions to members of the Order on training, public preaching at any opportunity, long periods of meditation, rest and sleep of course, availability for individual questions from gods or men, dialogue with opponents or with visiting dignitaries, and conversations with Ananda or other leading monks of the Order. A lot of this took place every day, except when on the move. A daily routine of this kind, slightly variable according to where he was or whether he

*Footprints of the Buddha. Drawing from
a 2nd century Amaravati stone relief*

was on the road, could produce an average, at a low estimate, of three expositions of teaching per day, not to mention incidental conversations. It is just this constant flow of teaching and exposition that had to be remembered and collected together which constitutes the original Dharma. On this basis the sheer volume of it was enormous., A simple (perhaps over-simple) calculation will give us an idea of its magnitude. Assume 3 expositions per day, more sometimes but repetitions would cancel these out. During retreat periods the instruction was intensified so a mean average of 3 per day is not untoward. Continue that rate of output over 45 years and we arrive at 49,275 expositions of varying length. Whether accurate or not, something of this order must have been the overall volume of the teaching. Of course, this takes no account of the type of teaching; whether in extended or condensed form, or with simple or complex content. Now this has not been a superficial exercise because it is an essential dimension of the Teaching *as given*; its great volume. One of the major traditions tells us that Ananda, when he was the Buddha's personal attendant, heard and remembered every word of teaching uttered and could recite it all together with detail of the place it was given, who it was given to, and in many instances the responses or the dialogue which accompanied each teaching. This is the basic idea behind the opening phrase of every sutra or sutta text; "Thus have I heard, at one time . . . etc." Ananda is held to be reciting each recorded event. For all the well known memorizing skills of the ancient (and some modern) Indian teachers, it stretches credulity that one man could recall every detail of such a vast body of verbal output at will. As we shall see later on, this is what is supposed to have happened at the first so-called Council at Rajagrha shortly after Sakyamuni's death. Ananda recited it all, the other arhats heard and remembered at first hearing and they passed it on down over all the intervening generations without omission or mistake. Well might we wonder at the feasibility of this. Indeed, some of the earliest matters of dispute within the Samgha concerned the possibility that the Ananda-line of recited recollections was incomplete in some respects. Again, this is not the place for critical appraisal. But it does lead us to select two of the stories to represent this vast 'open' period of Sakyamuni's life, as they are of some purpose in this presentation. The first story concerns Ananda himself.

It appears that, on one occasion while at Sravasti the Buddha declared that he was growing old and he needed a permanent attendant. Up to this point the monks of the Samgha had taken it in turn to attend him, to carry his bowl and robe, fetch him food and water when necessary and on occasion to regulate the press of visitors anxious to speak with him. This request for a permanent attendant seems to have happened in the 20th year of his ministry so he would have been about 55 years old. This is not an advanced age today but is suggestive of the wear and tear the incessant travel on foot must have produced. There is perhaps another reason hinted at in the record. One of his attendants is supposed to have disputed the right path to take on a particular journey. When

Sakyamuni insisted on one route his monk attendant simply put down the Master's bowl and robe and left him! This may reflect a situation where the post of attendant in rotation was not popular with all the monks for some reason. However it came about, the proposition was made. The first to volunteer was Sariputra. He was told that his work of teaching was too important and his offer rejected. Likewise other principal Arhats. Eventually Ananda offered himself under certain conditions. There were 8 of these and they included the receipt of alms and invitations, the presentation of visitors, the right to approach the Buddha whenever he wished and that any teaching given in his absence should be repeated to him. The content of the conditions is not surprising, but the fact that he made any at all is. At least it indicates a wish to avoid foreseen difficulties. All the conditions were accepted and Ananda thus became Sakyamuni's constant attendant for the remaining 25 years of his life. It was during this long period, over half of the Buddha's teaching span, that Ananda performed the task of listening to and remembering all the Buddha's teaching. It is odd however, that this was not one of the duties specified. Even so, what, we may ask, became of all the teaching given out in the first 20 years, before Ananda was in close attendance?

The second of our stories, which took place within the 'open' period, occurred before Ananda took up his familiar post. The incident occured among the monks of Kausambi, a city well to the west of the main Buddhist centres, on the River Yamuna. Here a dispute arose over a monk who was accused of an offence which he denied. Nonetheless he was expelled from the Samgha and immediately the local Samgha took sides as to the justification or otherwise of the sentence. After three months of dispute and wrangling the matter was still not settled and the Buddha was asked to intervene. When he arrived Sakyamuni pointed out how unseemly it was for those who had left the world to engage in quarrels like ordinary householders, but to no avail. One of our sources records that the monks said to the Buddha that he, as the 'Master of Law' could remain silent and above such matters, but they on their part could not refrain from replying when they were attacked. The Buddha was unable to reconcile the parties and so he rose into the air and retreated to a forest where he kept clear of the whole affair. Later, he went on to Sravasti where representatives from Kausambi sought him out to confess their intransigence. We are left to wonder at a case where even the direct particpation of the Buddha was insufficient to quell a relatively minor dispute which split a local Samgha into opposing factions. But there was worse to come.

As considerable comment has already been given in the body of this section, the only matter for concluding remark is the schism at Kausambi. If nothing else this incident indicates the growth of the Samgha to proportions where locations were self-governing, and by its very size would come to include elements incompatible with one another in certain places and in certain admixtures of membership. The Order of monks lead by the Buddha 'in person' was still a body of people afflicted by passions of one sort or another. It has to be expected that then, as now, the 'gates of the Immortal' were a long way off for the vast majority.

12) *Devadatta's schism, the Assembly at Anavatapta, and the deaths of Sariputra and Maudgalyayana.*

It will be recalled that Devadatta was a cousin of Sakyamuni and was of the Sakya nobility which joined the Order when Sakyamuni visited his family at Kapilavastu. It seems that by the time the Buddha was about 70 King Bimbisara of Magadha had been succeeded by his son Ajatasatru. In the meantime Devadatta had assiduously practised asceticism and had acquired the so-called magical powers of reproducing himself under any guise and wherever he wished. By a show of these accomplishments to Ajatasatru he won over his support and plotted to displace the Buddha, take the leadership of the Samgha and so, with Ajatasatru, gain spiritual and temporal control of the kingdom. Devadatta was ambitious and ruthless and had lost none of his Sakya pride of birth by his entry into the Samgha.

At first, Devadatta approached the Buddha and suggested that because of his advancing years Sakyamuni should relinquish the Order to him. On being refused Devadatta persisted until Sakyamuni addressed him in very severe and harsh terms; a rare occasion. At this, Devatta became angry and resolved to kill the Buddha. His first attempt at murder involved the placing of archers along a path frequented by the Buddha. But on the approach of Sakyamuni the archers found themselves unable to act, and so Devadatta resorted to direct action of his own. From a high cliff he threw down a large rock onto the Buddha walking below. Although the rock missed its mark some splinters broke off and one of these struck Sakyamuni's foot, drawing blood. Nothing daunted, Devadatta let loose a fierce elephant along a road into the city where the daily begging round took place. At the sight of the enraged elephant thundering down upon them Sakyamuni's accompanying monks fled, except for Ananda who placed himself in front of his Master to take the first shock of the animal's charge. The Buddha removed Ananda by his special powers and quietly proceeded on his way. As the elephant drew near his rage evaporated and he stopped and knelt down submissively in front of Sakyamuni.

Devadatta then resorted to the formation of a rival Order by stirring up controversy among the monks. He advocated the obligatory acceptance of five extra rules of rigorous discipline on all monks. Although this was rejected as compulsory (though always allowed voluntarily) Devadatta deceived several hundred monks into following him, thus creating a major schism. The Buddha sent Sariputra to persuade the break-away group to return, which they eventually did. Thus all Devadatta's schemes came to naught and he himself

soon fell fatally ill. Feeling his end approaching Devadatta asked to see the
Buddha again but Sakyamuni said that because of his deeds it would not be
possible. Devadatta came anyway to where the Buddha was, borne upon a
litter. Before he got within view however, the earth opened up and swallowed
him and he sank down to the lowest of the hells, Avici.

This story of Devadatta and the schism in the Order may indicate an actual
breakaway party which continued to exist independently after his demise. One
of our sources mentions an early record by the Chinese pilgrim Fa hien who
wrote of the existence of Devadatta's following, though whether we are to
understand that such a group was still present in Fa hien's time, c. 400 A.D., is
probematical.

Now as we approach the latter years of Sayamuni's life we find one of our
most venerable sources, part of the Vinaya of the Mulasarvastvadins of North
India, recounting the story of a strange foregathering of the Buddha and 500
Arhats, including Sariputra, on Lake Anavatapta. This semi-mythical lake was
located in the far north of India among the Himalayas. We are told that four
great rivers emerge from the lake and flow down to the plains. Access to this
lake for ordinary mortals is particularly difficult and perhaps for this reason the
gods made it a meeting place for their conventions. We shall see that the
assembling of the Arhats on Lake Anavatapta was for a specific purpose. Such
an assembly at this place was one of the 'ten indispensable actions' which every
Buddha has to perform during his life. It is a pattern of actions which was
known to the Pali commentators although the formal list of 10 does not appear
in the Pali texts. The ten items, which include several of the cardinal events of
the Life after the Enlightenment, also contain other features on which some
comment will follow at the end of this section. The list of ten necessary actions,
as recorded in one of the North Indian Vinayas and preserved for us in Sanskrit,
Chinese and Tibetan, reads (in translation) as follows:

The Ten Indispensable Actions of every Buddha.
(dasavasyakaraniyani)

The Bhagavat Buddhas do not enter Nirvana without remainder
before they have:
1. *Prophesied on the subject of the future Buddha.*
2. *Aroused in a living being a thought which does not turn away from the*
   supreme state of a fully and perfectly accomplished Buddha.
3. *Subdued all those who must be converted by him. (sarvabuddhavineyah)*
4. *Designated a 'pair of model disciples'. (sravakayuga)*
5. *Instituted a body of moral rules. (simabandha)*
6. *Fulfilled five sixths of a normal existence.*
7. *Performed a great miracle at Sravasti. (mahapratiharyam vidarsitam)*
8. *Been seen to descend from the heaven of the gods into the town of*
   Samkasya.

9. Established in the Truths (satyesu pratisthitam) his father and mother.
10. On the great Lake of Anavatapta, accompanied by the Assembly of disciples,
unravelled the web of past actions. (purvika karmaploti)

Item 10 of this list refers to the gathering on the Lake which concerns us now.

The account of this Assembly consists of the circumstances of the departure for the Lake and then, in the presence of the Buddha, 36 Arhats were invited in turn to explain to the whole gathering how his past actions in previous lives had played a decisive part in his present state of emancipation. In certain cases some tell how reprehensible behaviour in previous existences will continue to fructify even into the final phase of his last birth. As the whole sequence of stories cannot be given here a selection of representative instances will serve.

No indication is given of the period in Sakyamuni's life when this event took place but as it certainly occurred before the deaths of Sariputra and Maudgalyayana and as many of the best known Arhats make an appearance, it can be supposed that it too can be placed in the latter half of the great 'open' span of years mentioned above, though there is no certainty.

The story starts after the Buddha has preached to King Prasenajit of Kosala in his capital of Sravasti. Sakyamuni addressed his principal Arhats; 'Let us leave now for the great Lake Anavatapta where we shall unravel the web of our previous actions'. The Arhats assented and 500 of them accompanied the Buddha as they vanished from Sravasti and reappeared at the site of the Lake. As they all approached, many great lotuses rose from the centre of the lake so that the Buddha was able to alight and sit cross-legged on one while the 500 Arhats alighted and sat similarly on others. The first to open proceedings was Mahakasyapa who told the Assembly of his conduct in the past which had now produced a great fruit. He remembered in a long past existence how he saw an ascetic calm and dignified, and how he had a wish to emulate him. As he presented the holy man with a small measure of rough millet grains (all that was to hand) he also wished to meet more of such men in future. Mahakasyapa went on to explain that because of the power of that wish and gift he was reborn into the heaven of the 33 (Trayastrimsa) 1000 times over, then into a family of brahmins whence he left the world to follow the ascetic path himself. Finally he met Sakyamuni, joined the Order and became Arhat. He concluded by saying that all his wishes were realized and he had now gained his last birth.

After this first avowal the most senior among the Arhats then invited Sariputra in this manner; "What action has the Venerable Sariputra accomplished in order to become, thanks to the retribution (vipaka) of this act, so wise and skilful?' Sariputra responded with his story which is similar to Mahakasyapa's. He is followed by his companion Maudgalyayana, but here there is a difference. In the latter case he started by telling how, in a previous birth, he was so impressed by the demeanor of a local Pratyekabuddha that he formed a wish to become like him, like his predecessors. In consequence of the 'good root' he gained mainly heavenly and happy human rebirths. But once, when a young son of a merchant of Rajagrha he annoyed his parents who struck and reproached him. The boy felt anger and conceived the notion that he would like to beat his parents to pulp. Although he never actually carried out this youthful intention (though some say he did) he nevertheless suffered torment in the hell of the Black Chain (kalasutra) after that life expired. Even now, in his last birth as an Arhat renowned for his magical powers, he will suffer the final residue of that long past mental act by being himself beaten to death. Only then, on the exhaustion of all traces of retribution will he die and not be reborn again.

The others follow in turn, each being invited to ". . . unfold the thread of his karman . . ." In some cases relatively simple and mundane actions like sweeping clean a stupa courtyard with thoughts of respect, presenting a flower to a stupa similarly mindful, result in repeated favourable births until the fateful meeting with Sakyamuni and subsequent final release. In one case, the Arhat Vagisa tells how he enjoyed 90 kalpas of an unbroken sequence without a bad destiny. And all this was produced because of his gift to a stupa of some perfume, garlands and ointments which he had bought for the purpose with a few coins. Another case relates how, when the Arhat lived a previous existence as a rich merchant, during a period of famine a Pratyekabuddha begged at his door for food. In a fit of anger and avarice the merchant prepared poisoned food for him and he died on the spot. For this he endured long periods in various hot hells until he finally regained human birth. Even then, when he had met Sakyamuni and destroyed his passions he was still sickly and will remain so to the end.

The Arhat Upasena told how when he was a hunter he had shot and transfixed a seated Pratyekabuddha who had then died. Because of this he suffered thousands of years in the hells and as a wild animal roaming the mountains. Many times he was hunted and shot dead with arrows but still he returned to animal birth. Until one day his roaming brought him to a grove of penitent ascetics who, instead of chasing him away, sat and radiated light and calm. Thus confronted the animal experienced relief followed by feelings of respect and confidence in these humans. Because of the fruition arising from these thoughts, the animal regained human birth, met the Buddha and gained Arhatship. Even so, and despite his present purity, at the end of this his last life, he will enter a cave where a snake will bite him.

Our final example is unusual in another way. The Arhat Madhuvasistha related how in the distant past he was once a king of the monkeys, in the district of Vaisali. At that time there lived and preached in the area one of the previous Buddhas of the era. This monkey king used to squat at the top of a tree and listen to that Tathagata. Although he could not understand the words he was drawn to that Buddha and presented him with a gift of meal. That produced a human birth and a meeting with the present Buddha from whom he heard the Dharma, clearly this time, and 'gained the immortal'.

Even the Buddha himself is not immune from the doleful effects of the ripening of past causes. Another of our North Indian sources describes 9 mishaps or pains which Sakyamuni suffered which were direct results of past causes. These consist of false accusations, wounding in the foot by Devadatta, severe headache, poor or meagre food, starvation and bodily torture during his years of austerity, an aching back and excess of cold and heat. These ripening of past causes form the last section of the events at Anavatapta. Sakyamuni winds up proceedings by describing how the occasions when these incidents arose were all issued from his past existences.

We now come to the last year of Sakyamuni's life. It is at roughly this point that both Sanskrit and Pali texts pick up the consecutive narrative and carry the story to its final scenes with a wealth of detail and background. Forming a kind of prologue to the last act of this monumental drama are the circumstances of the deaths of Sariputra and Maudgalyayana, who both pre-deceased Sakyamuni by some months.

In the case of Sariputra, he took his leave of the Buddha knowing that his death would occur before that of his Master. Then he returned to his home village near Rajagrha to convert his mother and to die where he was born. Some monks went with him in attendance and lodged nearby. After establishing his mother in the first fruit of the Path i.e. Stream-entrant, Sariputra's sickness accelerated and at dawn, soon after his mother's attainment, he expired into final Nirvana. His attendant monks arranged and performed the funeral rites and then returned to Sakyamuni and the rest of the Samgha at Sravasti.

Only a short time after Sariputra's end his long time companion, Maudgalyayana also met his death. For Maudgalyayana however, the fructification of his past misdeed brought about a violent demise, quite unlike his friend's peaceful passing. Throughout his long life as an Arhat, Maudgalyayana's speciality had been in the wide ranging use of his magical powers (rddhi). Often he is described as visiting the realms of the gods and of the various hells to seek out, by his magical prowess, the place of rebirth of this or that one according to his actions. On 'returning' Maudgalyayana would relate to the Samgha just what had happened to this monk or to that heretic and the Buddha would moralize on the reported destiny for the benefit of the listening monks. Of course, this kind of activity did not long remain an exercise in private within the Samgha. Some monks would relate Maudgalyayana's exploits to their lay donors. In most cases, of course, the stories redounded to the honour of the Buddha's following and to the discredit of his religious opponents. At last some of the rival sectarians decided to remove this growing threat to their reputations. By a secret arrangement with local brigands they agreed to kill Maudgalyayana. Several times thereafter the bandits waylaid him on his rounds but each time he avoided them by rising into the air and removing to another place or by just vanishing. But as he himself knew and had recounted to his audience on Lake Anavatapta, nothing could prevent the retribution of his past acts and so finally, as the bandits persisted and his magical evasions weakened, they caught him at last and beat him to the point of death. With bones and muscles crushed Maudgalyayana was unable to move but he retained consciousness sufficiently long to create a 'mind-made' body, send it to where the Buddha was, and take his final leave. After this he expired and gained final Nirvana in just the manner he had himself foretold.

Thus departed the Buddha's two ablest and most eminent lieutenants. By their removal from the scene we are prepared for the departure of the central figure. For now with his advanced age Sakyamuni knew, as all Buddhas and Arhats know, the place and manner of his final entry into Nirvana. In the case of the Buddha Sakyamuni this closing episode of a long life is referred to as the Parinirvana.

We have already seen in section 11 that a minor disruption had already taken place in the Samgha before Devadatta's more serious challenge. In the latter case there was an actual rupture and some of the monks were drawn away to form a separate movement under Devadatta's leadership. In a mundane sense the story serves to illustrate that even such an other-worldly organization as a body of mendicant monks with the Buddha at their head was not immune to the effects of greed for power and prestige harboured by certain individuals. On the other hand the stories of a long surviving following of Devadatta may give us pause to wonder whether we have inherited a rather 'doctored' account by over-zealous monks whose only concern was to present Devadatta as a devil incarnate. However this may be, there is evidence for differing centres of gravity within the Samgha with traces in the Buddha's lifetime, and certainly immediately after his death. The so-called 'liberal' and 'orthodox' groupings which emerged in the first Councils suggest that such divergent views on certain aspects of doctrine and practice were in existence long before but largely held in check in deference to Sakyamuni's authority. In this light, it may be that Devadatta and others were simply impatient for change. Whatever the facts which underlie the ancient records it should not be overlooked that with such a large and widespread following, tensions were bound to be at work. Especially as that following had been drawn from all levels of the contemporary society from royal families to murderous brigands.

The account of the extraordinary convention at Lake Anavatapta and the list of '10 Indispensable Actions' which justify that gathering take us into a different realm of concern altogether. This scenario returns our thoughts to meditations on some of the inner significance of the sacred drama as a whole. In previous sections of this story we have seen that several of the principal characters (e.g. Sakyamuni's father and wife) had prepared the way in previous existences for the last act where they came together to fulfil clearly defined roles. The list of 10 Acts virtually sets out a series of obligations to be discharged by a Buddha before he passes into Parinirvana. They go some way in defining the 'role' of the Buddha himself. A glance at the list of 10 will show that they spread their concerns over the past, present and future. Some of them set the seal, so to speak, on past acts now brought to fruition. Nos. 4 and 9 concerning the 'model disciples' and his mother and father are of this type. Nos. 7 and 8 concern the present in that the Buddha is established as the spiritual overlord of this world-system; notice that both these incidents take place in public, for all to see. Also concerned with the present are Nos. 3 and 6 which ensure that everyone suitably endowed will have the opportunity to receive the Teaching and 'subdue' the passions. Also they set a minimum limit to the Buddha's human life span, though in the event Sakyamuni rejected a portion of what life remained to him, as we shall see. Nos. 1, 2 and 5 are obligations concerning the future. The moral rules for the firm foundation of the Samgha and the Way, are to be expected. In Nos. 1 and 2 however we seem to have a case of short and long term provision. For the (comparative) short term the next Buddha to come is named and located so that people are reassured that the immediate lineage is secure. But then No. 2 provides for a very long term indeed. The wording of No. 2 is very close to the idea of the Bodhicitta, the Thought of Enlightenment, which marks the commencement of the long career of the Bodhisattva. Certainly the intention appears to be the same; to launch at least one being on the Path which will eventually lead to the full Enlightenment of a Buddha in the far distant future. And yet this is part of a text belonging to a sect which was firmly rooted in the community of the Elders (Sthaviras) and nothing to do with Mahayana.

Finally, with No. 10 attention is directed toward the past to trace out the manner in which Arhats can themselves see how they have arrived at where they are. In a manner of speaking they are sacred dramas in miniature of the primary case of the Buddha himself. The same kind of distant chain of causes and conditions have been at work for them as for their Master and mentor. And not only do these 'unravellings of past karman' show how small seeds grow into great oaks, but they also show that bad as well as good actions ripen and deliver their results in long distant future periods. And surely these examples are intended for later generations to emulate. Simple causes bringing forth great fruits like gifts of food and sweeping out stupa courtyards are intended to encourage while the dire results of violent crime spell out the warnings. The biographies at the Lake taken together with the list of 10 can almost be seen as sketch-plans for a future re-run of the whole sacred drama with major and minor parts.

13) *The last journey and the Parinirvana.*

What was to be Sakyamuni's last earthly journey began at Rajagrha when, attended as usual by Ananda and a company of monks, he set out and headed north. His immediate destination was Vaisali, across the Ganges, and as was the custom the journey was made in several stages, stopping here and there on the way. Throughout this final journey the Buddha made several important pronouncements and he repeated and stressed to his monks some of the key features of the Doctrine. As well as speaking earnestly to his monks Sakyamuni addressed the local people who gathered to greet and to listen to him at every stop.

Before crossing the Ganges river he stopped on the south bank and observed building operations near a village. Sakyamuni foresaw the future greatness of that construction and told his listeners that one day what was then a-building would become a great capital city called Pataliputra, as indeed did happen before Asoka's time. After crossing the Ganges the party moved on northwards towards Vaisali. Before reaching that city two teaching statements were made. The first was to the monks in general about the need to attend to the Four Noble Truths. Now as we have seen earlier this was the subject of the first preaching at Benares and here again the Buddha repeats it as he must have done many times between. Here however, he told the monks that rebirth will continue for those who do not perceive and understand this cardinal teaching. Those who do perceive it, he said, will cut off the causes of suffering and for them there will be no more rebirth.

Further along the way Ananda asked about the destinies of those followers, monks and lay, who had died thereabouts. It seems that this had been a fairly frequent exercise but now the Buddha told him that in future he should use the formula called the Mirror of the Doctrine for this purpose. Anyone who maintained faith in the Three Jewels of the Buddha, the Dharma and the Samgha and who kept the moral rules unbroken was assured of freedom from rebirth into any of the lower realms of hell, animals or hungry spirits (pretas). The implied result in the contrary case was not explicit.

On arrival at Vaisali he stayed for a time and kept the seasonal retreat nearby. Here he fell seriously ill but used his special powers to restrain and suppress the sickness because he said it was not fitting for him to pass away before taking leave of the Order. Ananda, in close attendance, became very worried about Sakyamuni's condition and asked what was to be done about the Order after his Nirvana. The Buddha then told him that the whole of the Teaching had been given, what else was necessary for the Order? Using the title Tathagata, as he often did when referring to himself, the Buddha said that the Tathagata's body was old and like a cart held together with straps and ties, what more was expected of him now? Then he said to Ananda that they all should live as islands unto themselves having refuge in themselves and continued by saying that after his departure they would not be left without a Master. The Teaching

(Dharma) and the established discipline (Vinaya) should henceforth be their master.

Later on, still near Vaisali, Sakyamuni told Ananda that a Buddha has it in his power to live on for an aeon if he so wishes. In the Pali account Ananda did not grasp the implied invitation to request that he do so. After this Sakyamuni moved away from Ananda and sat apart. Mara then made another appearance, his last to the Buddha, and invited him to enter Nirvana straight away because all was accomplished. At this the Buddha said to Mara that indeed he would soon pass away into final Nirvana. Mara then left him, jubilant. At the moment of the rejection of the remaining life span the earth thundered and shook, firebrands lit up the sky and Ananda was petrified with fright. The point then dawned on Ananda and he hurried over to ask the Buddha to stay for his full term. But it was then too late. It has to be said that the Sanskrit version makes no mention of Ananda's tardy request or even of the Buddha's heavy hint beforehand. There, Sakyamuni voluntarily renounces his remaining term immediately after the request by Mara. Ananda is simply shown as being terrified by the earthquake and on asking the cause is told by the Buddha what he had just done.

Then Ananda was sent to assemble all the monks and the Buddha addressed them with the news that he will very shortly pass away into final Nirvana. He exhorted them with the phrase; impermanent are all composites, strive earnestly. After that the Buddha left Vaisali for the last time and as he reached the point on the northward road where the whole city could be seen, he turned his whole body around, as an elephant does, and gazed at Vaisali in farewell. Continuing the journey, now ever more slowly, they passed through various localities stopping frequently to rest, and at one of these the Buddha spoke of how, in the future, his followers could be sure what was true teaching. This became known as the formula of the Four Great Authorities and consists of:-

1. Teaching repeated by one who has heard that teaching from the Buddha himself.
2. Teaching repeated that was heard from the Elders of the established Samgha.
3. Teaching repeated that was heard from several learned Elders.
4. Teaching repeated that was heard from a single learned Elder.

In all four cases such teaching is to be checked with the Sutras (Scriptures) and with the Vinaya (Discipline). If such teaching is found there it is true Dharma; if not, it is not.

Journeying on further they came to the place of Cunda the smith. Here the accompanying monks were served with food by Cunda who, at the Buddha's request, served the 'pigs food' only to him. The other kinds of food were given to the monks. The exact nature of this 'pigs food' has been the subject of some debate but whatever it was the Buddha alone ate it and it was the last meal he had and he seemed to be well aware of the effect which was to follow. He insisted to Cunda that the remains of that dish should be buried. Soon after this Sakyamuni suffered a severe attack of pain and loss of blood. Despite this the party proceeded on its way but before long Sakyamuni had to rest near a stream. Ananda was sent to that stream for drinking water and although it was at first muddy and turgid, the waters cleared and ran pure for Ananda to take to the Buddha.

At last they arrived at Kusinagara and Ananda was asked to prepare a couch with robes with the head facing north. The Buddha then lay down on his right side with one foot on top of the other, in the so-called lion attitude. Nearby sal trees bloomed out of season and their flowers fell to cover his body. One of the attending monks stood in front of the Buddha fanning him and was told rather peremptorily to stand aside. This unusual brusque treatment prompted Ananda to ask why the monk should be spoken to so. The explanation was that myriads of gods were present all around them wanting to see the Buddha for the last time. There was no vacant spot even the size of the tip of a hair for miles around that was not occupied by watching gods and they complained that the monk blocked their view.

Ananda then asked for instructions regarding the funeral rites and was told that the ceremonies should be as for a 'wheel turning monarch' (Cakravartin) with a stupa accordingly. After this Ananda moved away to a quiet spot and there gave way to tears, not only because he was about to lose his dear Master but also because he still had not gained Arhatship. The Buddha sent for him and encouraged him to exert himself to attain the goal. He also spoke to the monks on how well and faithfully Ananda had attended him all the years. This seemed to restore Ananda's composure for he then said that surely this place of Kusinagara was too insignificant for the final Nirvana of a Buddha. He was told that though it was now small and unimportant the place had once been the capital city of a wheel turning king of a past age and so was entirely fitting.

Then Ananda was sent to the nearby clan of the Mallas to tell them the Buddha would pass away that very night so they could come to pay their last respects. Soon they arrived en masse and were presented in groups. Among them was an ascetic of the locality called Subhadra who asked if he could question Sakyamuni on some troublesome doubts. Ananda tried to dissuade him as time was limited but the Buddha overheard the exchange and invited Subhadra to question him. The answers he received convinced Subhadra and in no long time he gained Arhatship. He was thus the last convert to be made by the Buddha himself.

After settling several minor matters the Buddha addressed the assembled monks for the last time and ended his address with the exhortation he had used shortly before; ". . . impermanent are all composites, strive earnestly . . ." These were his last words. Then, watched with rapt attention by the assembled multitude of gods, members of the Order and local people, the Buddha, still lying on his side, entered the four absorptions (dhyana) one after the other. Ananda was moved to say to the Arhat Aniruddha standing nearby that the Lord had passed away. But Aniruddha corrected him by saying that the Lord had simply reached the stage of arrested consciousness. The final stages were closely observed and reported by Aniruddha who described how the Buddha passed back through the absorptions in reverse order and then, ascending them again passed into final Nirvana from the fourth. Again the earth shuddered and roared with thunder while violent winds raged and darkness deepened because of the sudden waning of the moon. Brahma, king of the higher gods, watching with his retinue, uttered a farewell verse. Likewise Sakra, king of the lower gods who was also present. The whole multitude, except for the Arhats, gave themselves over to grievous weeping. Mara and his hordes on the other hand, also watching the solemn event, were overjoyed. They danced and made a frightful din to celebrate the departure of their unconquerable opponent.

The Mallas took in hand the funeral ceremonies directed by the senior monks and the body was placed on a bier ready for cremation. When they attempted to light the fire it refused to burn. Aniruddha was again on hand to explain that the cremation could only take place after the arrival of Mahakasyapa and his party who were hurrying to the scene even now. While travelling in the direction of Kusinagara, Mahakasyapa had met a party of monks who had told him of the Buddha's decease. One of these monks is said to have remarked that there was no cause for grief. They were freed from the restraints of the Master and could now do as they wished. Mahakasyapa's disgust can be imagined but he hurried on to the funeral site and as soon as he had paid reverence to the bier it caught fire of itself and all was consumed. The rites were completed by a ceremonial distribution of the bone relics, which the Mallas conducted. The remains were divided into eight parts. Seven were shared among the rulers of nearby territories and one they kept for themselves. All the recipients of relics erected royal stupas over them for perpetual honour.

The date of the Great Decease generally accepted by modern scholars is 483 B.C.

Sakyamuni's long life came to a peaceful end. The traditions tell us plainly that he became weaker in his last years and that he had bouts of illness which he restrained until the final onset, brought to a climax by his last meal, carried him off at about his 80th. year. Here then is a very complex being. Acknowledged as their superior by the gods, yet not of their number. This Buddha or Tathagata, as he called himself, is not human either and yet follows the normal pattern of human life. His span of years, youthful appearance at the beginning of his ministry, aching weary limbs in advanced age, final expiry and cremation are all normal characteristics of human existence. But then, his special marks, superhuman powers and his own flat denial that he belonged to any of the levels of Samsara, leave us with something of an enigma.

He has been seen as such from the very begining. We are in excellent company in our uncertainty. Of all the major issues which occupied the entire Samgha in its early formative years, the nature of the Buddha was the most important. There were different, even contradictory opinions. The largest contingent of the Indian Samgha, formed after the first major dissension less than one and a half centuries after Sakyamuni's death, regarded the Buddha as an entirely supramundane being. All the events of his life from beginning to end were simply expedient means adopted to further the aims of the Teaching. His real existence was of infinite duration and his powers of transformation and adaptation were proportionately immense. And these were the views held by Indian Buddhist masters three centuries before the word Mahayana was even coined.

For us now, reading and pondering the traditional elements of the story it is fairly evident that we have a curious mixture of human characteristics, albeit of very high quality, and 'supernatural' features which dominate the record of how the Buddha referred to himself and which on special occasions were perceivable by others. In short, the records taken as a whole reflect the current notions about what he was not, but are tantalizingly vague about what he really was. The extreme subtlety of the earliest carved monuments which only show traces of the presence, can perhaps now be better appreciated. We are thus left to our own devices and there is a strong case for consulting the doctrinal records of the earliest schools for their informed perceptions before any of us jump in with ill-considered ideas of our own. In this re-statement of the ancient traditions on the Life, we are content to let the case rest as something of a mystery.

Some of the Buddha's recorded pronouncements on his last journey are of importance, especially those concerning the future regulation of the Order and the Teaching. First it should be noted that all the Teaching had been given. That teaching and the established discipline were to be regarded as the sure guide after the Buddha's death. These statements, and others, are the basis for the age-old concerns over the preservation and proper transmission of the Dharma and Vinaya to future generations.

Much the same can be said about the authoritative criteria for what is and is not valid Dharma. In an age when nothing of this kind was written down it was imperative to ensure that errors did not creep in. Indeed this was another of the major issues of the earliest Samgha. Then however, it was more a matter of what had been left out. Nowadays, although the written records of the Teaching are great in volume, we have a different version of this problem; the records we have are too little consulted, with the result that there is a great deal of personal opinion and not enough reference to the criteria we have been given.

A final comment concerns the monk who told Mahakasyapa that now the Master had gone they could do as they liked. If we add this incident to those of Devadatta's schism and the earlier rumpus at Kausambi, we can see some sign of the internal tensions of the Buddhist community already remarked upon in these pages.

14) *The Dharma recitations at Rajagrha*

The canonical texts of North India, preserved for us in Chinese, are now followed for the rest of the story. Elements of the same incidents are also preserved in Pali, but in the Northern records we have a continuous narrative.

Many of the Arhats living in seclusion in the forest or mountains were well aware of their Master's demise. A large number of them decided there was nothing further to be done now that Sakyamuni had completed his ministry. They too therefore, on their own volition, passed away into final Nirvana. The gods, observing the mass exodus of the remaining Arhats became disturbed and distressed. They thought and wondered who would be able to preserve and dispense the holy teaching so arduously gained by the Lord Buddha now that he is extinct and his leading disciples are also disappearing from the world? In some agitation certain of the gods approached Mahakasyapa and asked him if he knew what was going on. Was he aware, they said, that the lamp of the Dharma was going out in the world, that all the accomplished teachers and practitioners were abandoning the less fortunate? Before it was too late the Dharma must be firmly established for future generations. Mahakasyapa, thus prodded, perceived with his Arhat's vision that the gods were right and so he decided to gather the Teaching together. Accordingly he ascended to the top of Mount Meru and there struck the great gong. The sound reverberated widely throughout the world and carried with it Mahakasyapa's message to all the remaining Arhats. "Stay where you are! Do not pass into Nirvana! Remember the work of the compassionate Buddha! Beings yet to come will be lost and blind without the Eye of the Dharma! Wait until we have preserved his holy words and then pass into Nirvana if you will!" The Arhats obeyed and soon hundreds of them gathered with Mahakasyapa at their head near Rajagrha.

Mahakasyapa convened the meeting of the Arhats but Ananda was excluded because he still had not attained Arhatship. Their deliberations were soon halted because no one in the gathering could recall sufficient of the Teaching (Dharma). All agreed that Upali, the Sakyan barber, was able to recite all the Vinaya regulations and the circumstances that gave rise to them. When they considered who was capable of reciting the Dharma they first decided to call upon an Arhat called Gavampati, who had been a close companion of Sariputra. All the assembly agreed that Gavampati knew and could recite both Dharma and Vinaya but he remained in meditative retreat on the lower terrace of Mount Meru and had not responded to Mahakasyapa's call. So Mahakasyapa sent a messenger to Gavampati asking him to attend the Council and recite for them. When the messenger arrived and put his request to Gavampati he asked for confirmation that both the Buddha and Sariputra had passed away. On being told it was so Gavampati said that as the Buddha and Sariputra had gone he would not leave his retreat but he would follow them into Nirvana. Without further ado Gavampati rose into the air, performed the prodigy of fire and water after which he disappeared into Nirvana. The messenger could only return to Rajagrha with the news of his failure.

So no Arhat could be found who was able and willing to perform the recollection and the recitation of the Teachings. Ananda learned of the failure of the conference and put his mind to gaining the fruits of the Way so that he could be admitted to the august gathering. Throughout the whole night he sat in meditation, seeking fulfilment. At last he was exhausted and without success he lay down to sleep. As soon as his head reclined for sleep he was suddenly awakened to the fruits of the Way and thus acquired the diamond-like concentration so lacking hitherto. He then rapidly progressed to the destruction of all the passions and gained Arhatship. Quickly, he presented himself at the hall where the Arhats were gathered and banged on the door. When he learned it was Ananda at the door, Mahakasyapa told him to go away. Ananda protested that he was now an Arhat and qualified to attend. But Mahakasyapa (a hard man) replied that the door would remain closed and his only way of entry would be through the keyhole. Right! said Ananda, and exercising his new-won magical faculties he went in through the keyhole.

Then the whole gathering of Arhats including Mahakasyapa requested Ananda to recollect and recite the Teachings of the Buddha, which he did. Each incident and recitation being prefaced with the words; "Thus I have heard, at one time . . ." One of the texts of the Sanskrit tradition records that Ananda was also called upon to recite the groups of Dharma topics and extended explanations which came to to be known later as the Abhidharma. This he also did and so, together with Upali, all three collections of the Dharma were brought together. This triple division of the whole Scriptural corpus came to be known as the Three Baskets (Tripitaka), and is so known today.

Another of the contemporary Arhats, Purana, lived with his following a great distance away in the South. He too responded to the call but he did not arrive at Rajagrha until the whole proceedings were completed. He approached Mahakasyapa and asked if it were true that the Buddha had died and that the Elders of the Samgha had gathered to establish the Teaching. One of our sources tells how the Assembly asked Purana to accept the whole recitation as just collected. The other source recounts how the entire recitation was repeated for Purana's benefit. In both sources however, Purana asserted that he would hold to what he had himself heard from the lips of the Buddha. And there the matter rested.

Further consideration of how the enormous variety and volume of Sakyamuni's Teaching was recalled intact by one attendant and passed down to us word perfect and entire would lead us into the disturbed waters of controversy. But two of the incidents contained in this section are worthy of note. First there is the question of Ananda's recitation. In the 'northern' narrative which has been used, the body of Arhats in assembly chose Gavampati for the Dharma recitation and no doubt his close association with Sariputra had something to do with that. Had Gavampati agreed to recite the Dharma one imagines that his memory of the teachings were regarded as covering the entire span and not just over half as was the case with Ananda. Perhaps this was the reason why no one considered Ananda in the first place. The stated reason for his exclusion from the Assembly, not being an Arhat, could hardly have been decisive had he been the only one capable of the Dharma recollection and recitation. In this version of events then, Ananda was clearly a second choice, very probably because his access to the full range of the Teachings was incomplete.

The other incident; Purana's late arrival and insistance on holding to what he had himself heard from the Buddha, is remarkable in that it occurs in both the major traditions. Here we have a strong suggestion of some well remembered teaching or instruction which was not contained in that first recitation at Rajagrha. Whether the omission was small or large is of no account compared to the significance of there being something missing, or felt to be so. It is little to be wondered at that there was anxiety and concern in those early years after the Buddha's death as to whether the recited canon at Rajagrha was complete in all respects. And this concern was to surface on several occasions when arguments and controversy about other matters led to a major division within the Samgha. When this happened the two separate wings added to or amended the recited canon according to their views of what was right and proper. From then on further fragmentation took place and the several main Buddhist communities were free to incorporate into their own Dharma recitations those parts which had either been disputed by other groups or were unknown to them. Thus to gain access to the whole range of remembered teaching in all its variety one has to take account of the canonical records of all the earliest mainland Indian Buddhist schools and not just the one which has become the best known in the modern West. All that having been said, matters would have been far less difficult if only Gavampati had agreed to come down from his mountain and recite.

15) *Mahakasyapa awaits the next Buddha: Maitreya*

With the Dharma teachings recited and consigned to the collective memory of the Arhats in attendance at the Rajagrha assembly, Mahakasyapa decided he could take his leave. No doubt some of his colleagues came to the same decision, especially if Mahakasyapa's order to convene at Rajagrha had prevented them from passing away into Nirvana beforehand. The North Indian texts continue the story.

One morning, after completing his usual begging round in Rajagrha, Mahakasyapa retired to Vulture Peak (one of the city's encircling mountains) and told the other monks that he would that day pass away. Some of those monks quickly went into the city and informed the leading citizens. They were aghast at the news. As they said, first it was the Lord Buddha himself who departs, then large numbers of his Arhats were only restrained from doing the same by the example of Mahakasyapa. Now he is going too. They were very sad and downcast.

At dusk all the monks and the townspeople gathered on the slopes of Vulture Peak to pay their last respects, witness Mahakasyapa's departure and perform the funeral rites of cremation. But they were about to witness the utterly unexpected. In the cool evening Mahakasyapa emerged from his customary meditations and sat down in front of the gathering. He then preached to them on the universality of impermanence, on the painful nature of all existence, and on the total lack of substance in anything (the formula of the Three Signs or Seals). On completing his homily he took up his cloak, given to him by Sakyamuni, his bowl and staff and suddenly rose into the air. There, high above the heads of the assembly he performed the prodigy of fire and water, just as the Buddha had done before him. Fire and water poured out from his body in all directions. Afterwards he descended to the mountain top and uttered a solemn promise that his body would not decay until the next Buddha, Maitreya appeared. With that he turned and entered the rock of the summit ". . . as if he was going into soft mud . . ." After he had disappeared into the mountain the summit closed over him with solid rock. Within the mountain Mahakasyapa sank into the deep meditation of the 'stopping of consciousness' and will remain thus, undisturbed, as if sleeping until the Buddha Maitreya shall come to awaken him.

In the distant future when the next Buddha gains full Enlightenment in the world, exactly as Sakyamuni did in the past, human beings at that future time will have a life span of thousands of years and will stand 80 feet high. The Buddha Maitreya himself will stand 160 feet high with limbs and features proportionate. He will convert and discipline innumerable beings but, in general, the people of that time will be lazy and loath to exert themselves. Perceiving this fault, Maitreya will come to Vulture Peak at Rajagrha. He will strike the summit a blow and this will awaken Mahakasyapa who will then emerge from the rock. His body will be whole and his faculties intact. Carrying his cloak, bowl and staff, he will prostrate at Maitreya's feet and hand over to him the cloak. He will say to Maitreya that this cloak was entrusted to him by Maitreya's predecessor. Once the cloak has been accepted Mahakasyapa will again rise into the air and perform the prodigy of fire and water before Maitreya and the astonished eyes of his entourage and the people. This time however, on completing the fire and water 'pairs' he will destroy his body and disappear into Nirvana.

Maitreya's disciples and all the onlookers will then be curious and they will ask Maitreya, "Who is that miniature man dressed as a monk and how is it he can perform such extraordinary feats?" They will then hear the story of how he was a premier disciple of the previous Buddha, how he ensured the precious Teaching was conserved after the Parinirvana, and how he has waited within the mountain until the next Buddha appeared. And all this, says Maitreya, was accomplished by a man who lived in a difficult age when humans were tiny and had only a short time to live. Turning the story into an appropriate teaching device for his followers, Maitreya will tell them that the previous Buddha Sakyamuni has seen them all. It was he who set them on the path to deliverance but they have had to await the coming of Maitreya before they could attain it. Now they have seen with their own eyes what such as Mahakasyapa had achieved. Even with a tiny body such great feats are possible, so why should not they with large bodies and correspondingly superior faculties do the same?

Thus the next Buddha Maitreya, having released Mahakasyapa and induced shame in his assembly, will teach the Dharma and enable many to attain quickly the fruits of the Way. And those who quickly attain will have been launched and guided onto that Path by Sakyamuni in a previous age. Others, on seeing such wonders and hearing the Teaching from the lips of Maitreya will plant 'good roots' for their advantage in future ages still.

Such is the story, in its full span of past, present and future, of the appearance and the passing of the last Buddha Sakyamuni and the coming appearance of the next Buddha Maitreya. Although much has had to be omitted the outline and the major elements of the various traditions are here represented in approximate sequence. All that remains is to complete the comment on this last section.

The story now completed, or rather left at a certain point, it can be seen that no end to the great drama is intended. Many strands of past events and past lives were drawn together around Sakyamuni's earthly life and after his death many other ingredients were gathered and transmitted onward with care and concern. Even a direct individual continuity is preserved by Mahakasyapa's wait to deliver the cloak to Maitreya. There is no doubt that Maitreya will follow the age-old precedents. How can there be an end to such a story? And how well these ancient traditions deserve their designation as sacred literature, to be treated accordingly.

Now, in Part II of this Booklet we retrace our steps to the first Teaching at Benares, and the chance to plant 'good roots'.

THE BUDDHA AS PHYSICIAN
THE DHARMA AS MEDICINE

1) *Preliminaries*

It has already been shown that the traditional Biography of Sakyamuni contains strong elements of the Dharma or Teaching. In the Biography those elements are intertwined within the story though they can be unravelled as the Arhats did their karman on Lake Anavatapta. Now we turn our attention to the Teaching as such, the records of what the Buddha said, expounded and explained as remembered and preserved by the Buddhist masters of India and Ceylon within the mainstream consensus previously described. That teaching is expressed at great length in the sutras and commentaries. Our concern here is to present the fundamentals of that teaching as plainly as possible. For that purpose the ancient technique of concentrating the main subjects into formulas is entirely suitable. The first and perhaps the primary formula of all is the one called the 'Four Noble Truths'. It will be recalled that this was the subject of the first turning of the Wheel at Benares (Part I section 9) and it was preceded by the pronouncement of the Middle Way.

Although this formula of the Four Noble Truths was the first expressed teaching of Sakyamuni Buddha to the world it should not be thought of as elementary, in the sense of easy or simple. It was the result of deep pondering under the Bodhi tree on how to express the inexpressible; how to convey the Buddha-knowledge to the worldly. It should also be remembered that this particular teaching was delivered to a selected few to start with, who were judged to be the most suitable to receive the new doctrine. So it represented something of a part-way stage between the full Buddha-knowledge of the Enlightenment and conventional wisdom on the one hand; and another kind of part-way stage in that it was addressed, not to 'ordinary' people but to experienced ascetics who had already left the worldly life but were deeply enmeshed in wrong views about the ultimate goal, on the other hand. In short, the formula itself is a veritable 'middle Way'.

As we have seen in Part I the gaining of full Enlightenment requires vast amounts of continuous development and favourable conditions. The Buddha saw that the unobstructed knowledge of 'true nature' was beyond the capacities of unprepared beings. First of all the hardened crust of impurity had to be at least partly removed and a new outlook adopted before the 'deep, subtle and transcendental knowledge' could be accessible. In this connection a favourite simile of the Buddha was the example of the man pierced by an arrow. Such a man would be foolish to start a detailed enquiry into who fired it, from which direction, and so on. The immediate need is to remove it. Causes, reasons and everything else can wait until the wound is treated, otherwise the patient will die and both the questions and answers will be tragically irrelevant. Such a supposed situation explains why the Buddha is sometimes called the Great Physician who knows the nature of the disease or wound, who reassures the patient that a cure is possible, and who sets about the requirements of the cure first and foremost. This was just the position at the time of the First preaching, and it remains so. The formula of the Four Noble Truths presents us with the fact of the universal disease, that there are causes for it, and a cure. The cure requires a number of specific medicines which should be applied at once.

2) *The basic formula of the Four Noble Truths (aryasatya)*
Here then is the formula in its concise form:-
i.   All existence is suffering (duhkha).
ii. The true origination of suffering has been discovered (samudaya).
iii. The stopping of that suffering is possible (nirodha).
iv. The Way leading to the stopping of suffering is 8-fold (marga).

Regarded in the light of the simile of the Great Physician these four Truths are described thus:-
The first truth of suffering specifies the disease.
The second truth of the origination shows the cause of the disease.
The third truth of stopping is the cure.
The fourth truth of the Way or Path is the medicine which cures.

Thus the basic formula which summarizes the true situation as seen by an Enlightened Buddha and expressed with a view to convincing unenlightened people of the prevalent sickness and pointing out the means of restoring full health.

3) *The brief meanings.*
The pronouncement itself was actually made in rather more detail, though even here in a quotation from the texts there is much not readily grasped at first sight:-
What then monks is the Noble Truth of Suffering?
Birth is suffering, decay is suffering, sickness is suffering, death is suffering; to be in situations one does not like is suffering, the separation from what one likes is suffering, not to get what one wants is suffering; in short the five groups of the grasping/clinging personality (upadanaskandha) are suffering.

What then monks is the Noble Truth of the origination of suffering?
It is the craving/thirst (trsna) which gives rise to rebirth, together with pleasure and greed which seeks delight here and there; the craving/thirst

for sensual pleasure, the craving/thirst for further existence, the craving/ thirst for non-existence.

What then monks is the Noble Truth of the stopping of suffering? It is the extinction of that craving/thirst, renouncing it, forsaking it, liberation and detachment from it.

What then monks is the Noble Truth of the Way which leads to the stopping of suffering? It is the Noble Path in eight parts, namely:- Right View, Right Intentions, Right Speech, Right Action, Right Livelihood, Right Effort, Right Mindfulness, Right Concentration.

It was in this form that Kaundinya heard it and became the first of the five disciples to realize the liberating truth of what it really meant. The other four took a little longer and no doubt it was a further expansion of the formula which occupied them during the intensive period of instruction that followed.

4) *Expanded meanings.*

The necessary elaboration of this highly concentrated formula resulted in what came to be known as the 16 Aspects of the Four Noble Truths i.e. each of the four truths had four kinds of subsidiary meanings:-

i.   The truth of Suffering (duhkha).
    a) because the very nature of existence is painful.
    b) Because of the dependence of all things on causes.
    c) because of emptiness; nothing lasts.
    d) because impersonal; no real self can be found.

ii. The Truth of Origination (samudaya).
    a) is the cause because seeds of past actions become causes.
    b) is the origin because manifestation is due to immediate causes.
    c) is production because of a series of successive appearances.
    d) is conditions because of the concurrence of a variety of conditions.

iii. The Truth of Stopping (nirodha).
    a) is cessation because the personality groups (skandhas) are extinguished.
    b) is calm because greed, hatred and delusion are extinguished.
    c) is sublime because no calamity can occur.
    d) is escape because there are no further causes of pain.

iv. The Truth of the Path (marga).
    a) is the Way because one travels it toward Nirvana.
    b) is the correct method because it is effective and supplied with means.

c) is security because it leads to Nirvana.

d) is release because it produces a final exit into the beyond.

A definition was also given of each of the eight factors of the Path, thus:-

Right view is the knowledge of the Four Noble Truths.

Right Intentions is the intention not to harm or hurt.

Right Speech is refraining from falsehood, malicious, harsh or frivolous speech.

Right Action is refraining from taking life, from stealing and from sexual misconduct.

Right Livelihood is gaining a living by proper means.

Right Energy is stopping bad thoughts arising and dispelling those already present. Production of good thoughts not yet arisen and sustaining those already present.

Right Mindfulness is mindful attention to the body, feelings, the mind and dharmas.

Right Concentration is to attain and abide in the Four Absorptions (dhyana).

5) *The formula as focus of practice and the formula of practical technique.*

In all the early Indian Buddhist schools this basic formula (and others) was held to reveal more of its Enlightenment content as one progressed in the practice of its penetration. For the Way was always understood to be gradual. Understanding, revelation and release were acquired by stages. One well known text, the Dhammapada, puts it thus;

Let a wise man blow off his own impurities, as a smith blows off the impurities of silver, one by one, little by little, and from time to time.

The same theme occurs many times in the texts. It is just this way with the Four Noble Truths. The expanded meanings and the 16 Aspects illustrate the growth or depth derived from the original formula. At some point in the early Indian development the process was formalized into a 5 stage passage leading to Nirvana. The detail of the 5 stages will be explained in a later Booklet. Now, in connection with the Four Noble Truths, the middle stage of the 5 consists of a profound penetration of the formula similar to Kaundinya's experience, which conveys an absolute conviction of its verity and a direct perception of its operation. It is recorded that this experience was so moving that the meditator sometimes gave an involuntary cry; 'Oh what sufering'. This middle stage is known as the Way of Vision (darsanamarga) and its name suggests what is involved. The Abhidharma texts refer to this 'visionary' perception as a 'comprehension' (abhisamaya) and the whole process is surprisingly brief. It consists of only 16 thought moments but each of these is very highly charged. The 16 thoughts are directed upon the 16 Aspect version of the formula in a particularly powerful manner. By means of eight pairs of moments, one a realization (ksanti) and one a knowledge (jnana) full comprehension of each aspect is gained and all doubt is destroyed. This is followed in series by the destruction of the gross passions of greed and hatred as well as the certain knowledge that one is released from them.

This stage of 'vision' marks the entry into the Path proper. Final Nirvana can then be reached in a maximum of seven more births. Thus the stage of darsanamarga is also called 'Entry into the Stream' (srota-apanna). The deep penetration to realization of the full meaning of the Four Noble Truths just described is a prime example of the conjunction of Teaching and Practice which is characteristic of the Dharma as a whole. In this case we have a visionary grasp of the content of doctrinal formulations which give rise to positive, marked progress in the Way of extrication from the 'fires' of greed, hatred and delusion.

Another brief formula comes into play here. As all the major doctrinal formulas, like the Four Noble Truths, are examples of the inter-dependence of Teaching and Practice, they are meant to be opened out and explored as a means of obtaining insight (prajna) and that special comprehension (abhisamaya) of their essence which destroys doubts and destroys certain categories of defilements (klesa). The brief formula which describes how that is to be done consists of just 3 Sanskrit words;

1. To listen to (or read) the Teaching attentively (sruta).
2. Then to ponder and consider what one has heard (cinta).
3. Then, to apply to all that meditative concentration (bhavana).

This is the key practice technique which applies throughout the whole range of the Dharma, Mahayana as well as mainstream. The words of the discourse or of the formula have to be listened to (or read) with maximum attention and taken to heart. Their meaning and import then have to be mulled over, weighed, compared with experience and carefully considered. Finally, the acute and sustained concentration (samadhi) developed by meditation practice has to be directed upon a distillation of all that until the inner meaning unfolds and the formula reveals its liberating insight. That revelation is what propels the practitioner along the Path.

Here we have one of the primary reasons for careful attention to the terminology and for the preservation and transmission of the Dharma texts. The words and phrases, especially in the formularies, are parcels and packages containing the real meaning of the Teaching. Part of the proper practice is to focus on these parcels until they open up. Thus the Teaching or Doctrine and the Practice in dynamic cooperation produce progress in the Path.

6) *Two Phases of Gradual Progress*
Of course the deep penetrative meditation of the Teaching and Entry into the Stream is an advanced stage. Yet it is open to all and some may be fitted to approach it because of their karmic inheritance, but intense and sustained

application is required and so efforts of this kind are usually reserved for the cloister. The Way is indeed gradual but there is a 'fast gradual' and a 'slow gradual'.

The 'fast gradual' is the rapid cure of the man wounded by the arrow. It consists of the removal of the arrow and the closing of the wound. By the nature of the process that can be painful and is best performed in the ideal circumstances of a sterilized operating theatre. The 'fast gradual' or the rapid cure was regarded by all the mainstream schools as the province of the monk or nun under close instruction. For such a candidate embarking on the approach to the Way proper, his instruction and mode of life centred upon three major elements — another formula:-

  i. Strict moral conduct (sila).

  ii. Developing skill in one-pointed concentration (samadhi).

  iii. Gaining access to insight-wisdom (prajna).

The first of these three, sila, is the foundation stone on which rests the whole structure of the Teaching/Practice combination. For the monk actually beginning this 'cure' his strict moral conduct and detailed discipline is meant to detach him from superfluous involvements and the cardinal passions and defilements once and for all. By accepting these disciplines and regimen from the start the natural turbulence and compromise of everyday worldly life are put aside so as to produce a degree of calm and mental clarity. This basis of strict sila acts as support and condition for the refinement of concentration which can then be directed to the assembly of formulas or Teaching 'packages'. He thereby takes hold of the 'packages' and begins to unravel them. This concentration in its turn becomes the initial element of the insight-wisdom (prajna) which actually penetrates to the inner contents and by probing the embedded arrow enables it to be finally dislodged.

For the general majority, the less hardy or those more closely circumscribed by their inherited circumstances, the 'slow gradual' approach is prescribed by the Great Physician. For the wounded man of this kind, it is a case of alleviation of pain, breaking off the arrow shaft to prevent aggravating the wound, and reducing the fever. It also involves finding shelter from exposure to further arrow wounds. The removal of the arrow head has to be postponed until the fever abates and strength is restored. For them another formula applies;

  i. Generosity and supporting activity (dana).

  ii. Basic moral conduct (sila).

  iii. Consolidating the conditions for a favourable rebirth (svarga).

This majority is the community of lay-followers, those who recognise and accept the Lord Buddha as their guide, his Dharma or Teaching as their torch to illuminate the Way and who help and support those 'fast runners' who precede them. These are the traditional Three Jewels of Buddha, Dharma, Samgha, which are the shelter within which all, monks and lay alike, take refuge. By generous giving and other good actions the lay-follower sets in train the development of future happy and fruitful conditions for himself. By the practice of basic moral conduct they avoid falling into the lower destinies at death and in the present they reduce their 'fever' and prevent exposure to further arrow wounds. They look to a later opportunity for gaining full recovery when the ripening of conditions opens up the possibility of switching to the 'fast track' of the rapid cure. A good example of this form of teaching to lay people, as employed by the Buddha himself is given in Booklet No. 1 page 33 where the case is likened to a gambler who makes a 'lucky throw'. The lay majority also looked to the 'achievers' on the 'fast track' to witness for them that the Path was indeed attainable and that it actually produced the results claimed for it.

These two groups of practitioners with their different codes of conduct; the totally devoted candidate for the Path proper who has 'gone forth', and the faithful householder supporters who keep them in the basic necessities and who observe their progress for encouragement and inspiration; these two groups formed the basis for the traditional mutually dependent wings of the Samgha. That is how it always was and how it remained in all the Samghas of Asia for many centuries.

7) *The Three Signs or Seals of the Dharma*

The long vistas conjured up by the teaching of many successive Buddhas also emphasises another crucial matter. Many times we find the statement that each Buddha re-discovers the ultimate truth which is always there but unperceived and unreachable until a Buddha re-opens the Way. There are passages in the texts where the Buddha speaks to his monks concerning this and where he expresses something of the Enlightenment experience itself. These sections often contain enigmatical phrases which should not now surpirse us bearing in mind the nature of full Enlightenment and the difficulties involved in expressing, let alone teaching, what took place under the Bodhi tree. One such statement, whose few words belie its depth of meaning, is found repeated in the Pali canonical texts as well as in certain primary Mahayana sutras:-

Whether Saints appear in the world or not, the true nature of things (dharmanam dharmatā) is always present.

Even a casual reading of this brief quotation shows it to be very close to an absolute statement about 'true nature'. It also expresses in just two Sanskrit words what it is that Buddhas re-discover. No wonder these enigmatical remarks occupied the attention of Buddhist masters for ages. This 'true nature' is the very stuff and essence of all the Teaching and the revealing of it for each one of us is the ultimate goal and purpose of all practice.

Such statements are not, like the Four Noble Truths, pitched to a particular level of listener. They are much closer to the heart of the matter and to things as they really are, and so they do not have a practical dimension at all. Therefore when we find the same absolute style of expression being used for a statement on the 'true nature' of things which is also linked to the practical formula of the Four Noble Truths, we can be sure it is of more than usual importance. Such a statement, also brief, is again to be found in the Pali canonical texts:-

Whether Perfect Ones appear in the world or whether Perfect Ones do not appear in the world, it still remains a firm condition, an immutable fact and fixed law: that all formations are impermanent, subject to suffering and impersonal.

Comparing the two extracts it is obvious that the opening phrases about Perfect Ones (or Saints) appearing in the world are variant translations of words which, in the original language, are the same in both cases. They are followed by the absolute mode as in the words "... always present ..." and "... immutable fact ..." In the case of the latter extract these 'immutable facts' came to be regarded as the hallmark or special characteristics of the Dharma as such. As with so many of the main teachings this statement was later rendered as a formula and in so doing the clarity and precision of the original was emphasized. Here is the basic formula with the original Sanskrit added as it appeared in a variety of early texts:-

All composites are impermanent.
(sarve samskara anityah)

All composites are suffering/turbulent.
(sarve samskara duhkha)

All the elements are without a Self.
(sarve dharmah anatmanah)

Nirvana is peace.
(santam nirvanam)

In the Sanskrit versions the fourth line on Nirvana is added, firstly to make this concise statement a complete representation of the Dharma as a whole, and secondly, to complete the inner logic of the meaning. As in previous cases the formula needs to be opened out. The difference here is that each line leads into the next, as we shall see.

8) *Inter-linked meanings of Major Formulas*

In general terms, and in our parlance, this formula means:-
1) Everything and everyone changes incessantly (anityata).
From the atom, up through mankind and the physical world to the stars and the nebula, all is in process of change. This is usually perceived or conceived of as happening slowly and we sometimes call it development or evolution.

In fact, close analysis by instrumentation or by inward reflection shows that the change is actually brought about by moment to moment displacement or inter-action of small constituents. For example, the shape of a cloud changes slowly, swelling or constracting and propelled en masse by the wind. What is really happening is that the constituents of the cloud, water particles etc., are moving and combining rapidly and it is their condensation and evaporation which determine the shape and the very existence of the cloud itself.

This brings us to a rather more precise perception. It is that everything and everyone is a composite (samskara) i.e. made up of a variety of basic elements. Because it is the nature of these basic elements to have a short life and give way to others, equally short lived, the composite as a whole changes. But the change in fact takes place at the rate of its constituent elements, moment to moment. Thus the change involves the loss of one combination to be replaced imperceptibly by another, ad infinitum.

ii) We are led straight to the second of the Signs or Seals. This incessant change i.e. replacing certain things with others, the deaths of some, the births of others, results in a general turbulence or commotion, described in the texts as the birth, growth, decline and death of all phenomena. We may very properly recall at this point the full meaning of the word Samsara, which includes just this. The birth, growth, decline and death, the constant arc of existence, necessarily applies to everyone and everything. And it continues unabated into infinity. The Arena and its Performers are a non-stop show. Thus the turbulence, the churning, the incessant change goes on without a break and beyond any control. So, outwardly, 'all composites are turbulent' (duhkha). Inwardly too, the composites are turbulent, not only because our constituents describe the universal arc, but also because the very condition of turbulence produces suffering (duhkha). What we like disappears and what we dislike reappears. What we like sometimes comes back again, but it soon goes and the perpetual turmoil gives rise to constant loss and consequent instability. Here we are involved in an extended version of the first and second Noble Truths, and it is a clear example of how these main teaching formulas interlock with each other. The penetration of one leads into the others and we find ourselves moving through a highly integrated series of formulas, each of which contains insights of similar flavour.

iii) With the third Sign or Seal the change of subject from composites (samskara) to elements (dharmas) is significant but is sometimes lost or obscured in an English translation. Under the third Sign the formula treats of the little wretches that actually cause the change, the turbulence and the suffering; the constituent elements (dharmas) themselves. Remember that the composite is what it is because of the combination of its elements. The composite is only how a conglomerate of elements appears to ones view. The cloud is simply the outward and visible shape that its constituent elements assume from moment to moment. In concentrated inward introspection, or in microscopic analysis of the physical organism, the elements are seen as in constant flux, no part ever at rest for a moment. Body and mind are alike in this, that they are both in a perpetual state of modification. In this respect they only differ in the *rate* of change, in the speed at which the change takes place. An inkling of what is going on can be gained if we stop and observe objectively what goes on in our own heads. But even here, the intensity and the quality of the observation change. If we want to sustain the observation it soon has to be buttressed by other elements, like the will. And here, we reach the inter-related third Sign. Because the elements of the body and mind, as with all else, arise and pass away so remorselessly, there is no permanent, central, unchanging Self (anatman). There is no entity or inner core around which all the change revolves. There is no heart-stuff or substance to which everything else happens or which possesses qualities in process of change, while it remains central, stable and receptive. In short, there is no soul or Self which moves intact through life being affected by experience and eventually passing out of the body intact for more of the same somewhere else. What there is, is an unstable mix of all the active elements, changing or being displaced momentarily, but preserving temporary forms and feelings. As long as the constituents (dharmas) repeat a certain pattern, the form or the appearance, the composite (samskara) preserves a nominal identity. The shape of the cloud illustrates this well. The outward shape has a 'character'. There are storm clouds and summer clouds and those with silver linings. The fundamental reality of their composition remains the same . . . total and constant flux.

All three Signs are brought together in a single teaching exposition by the Buddha when he explained to his monks how this state of affairs should be dealt with.

What do you think monks? Is bodily form and sense impressions (rupa) permanent or impermanent? Impermanent Lord, they replied.

Are feeling 'vedana), perception (samjna), mental composites (samskara) and consciousness (vijnana), permanent or impermanent? Impermanent Lord, they replied.

But what is impermanent, is that pleasant or the cause of suffering (duhkha)? It is suffering Lord, they replied.

But of that which is impermanent, suffering and subject to change, when that is considered could one rightly say; This belongs to me, this is me, this is my Self? No Lord, they replied.

Therefore, whatever there is of bodily form etc, (as above first para.) whether past or present, or future, internal or external, gross or subtle, far or near, there one should understand according to reality and true wisdom: This does not belong to me, this is not me, this is not my Self.

Once again this is an extended formula which is meant to be penetrated so as to reveal its liberating insight. It is a formula which combines Teaching and Practice in high degree and so is a proper candidate for the exercise of that special technique of listening (or reading), considered pondering as a prelude to meditative concentration. It is hardly to be wondered at that the formula of the Three (Four) Signs or Seals came to be regarded as a comprehensive summary of mainstream Teaching as a whole. Entry into its underlying meanings and application lead into other formulas of Teaching and Practice, and eventually with the gaining of insight/wisdom into proximity with 'the nature of things'.

In the next Booklet, No. 3, we move somewhat closer to the great wisdom of the full Enlightenment. There we shall consider some of the special formulas of advanced practice including the king of all formulas, the Pratityasamutpada, 'Arising due to Conditions'. This formula summarizes, or tries to, the very essence of the Buddha's supreme insight into the world process. In addition to that the third Booklet will contain an exposition of the Buddhist doctrine of Karman. Once more the ancient texts will be called upon to explain a topic which is rarely treated in any detail in Western interpretations of the Dharma.